KETO FAT BOMBS COOKBOOK

Quick, Easy and Healthy Ketogenic Fat Bomb Recipes

(Ketogenic Fat Bomb Recipes for Weight Loss)

Naomi Wherry

Published by Sharon Lohan

© Naomi Wherry

All Rights Reserved

Keto Fat Bombs Cookbook: Quick, Easy and Healthy Ketogenic Fat Bomb Recipes (Ketogenic Fat Bomb Recipes for Weight Loss)

ISBN 978-1-990334-21-4

All rights reserved. No part of this guide may be reproduced in any form without permission in writing from the publisher except in the case of brief quotations embodied in critical articles or reviews.

Legal & Disclaimer

The information contained in this book is not designed to replace or take the place of any form of medicine or professional medical advice. The information in this book has been provided for educational and entertainment purposes only.

The information contained in this book has been compiled from sources deemed reliable, and it is accurate to the best of the Author's knowledge; however, the Author cannot guarantee its accuracy and validity and cannot be held liable for any errors or omissions. Changes are periodically made to this book. You must consult your doctor or get professional medical advice before using any of the suggested remedies, techniques, or information in this book.

Table of contents

Part 1 1
INTRODUCTION 2
Chapter 1: 14 Useful drinks you should know 5
1. Smoothie 5
2. Po Cha 7
3. Creamy Coconut Smoothie 9
4. Creamy Mexican Hot Chocolate 11
5. Eggnog Smoothie 13
6. Gingerbread Gem Smoothie 15
7. Key Lime Pie Smoothie 17
8. Matcha Madness Smoothie 19
9. Peanut Butter Cup Smoothie 21
10. Amaretto Chilled Coffee 23
11. Vanilla Smoothie 25
12. Vanilla Avocado Smoothie 27
13. Vanilla Almond Butter Smoothie 29
14. Strawberry Vanilla Smoothie 31
Chapter 2: How to have a delicious dish quickly and easily .. 33
15. Salted Caramel Almond 33
16. Mocha Ice Bombs 35
17. Low Carb Frozen Chocolate Chip Balls 37
18. Valentine's Day Keto Fat Bombs 39
19. Ice Cream 41
20. Blueberry Cheesecake Popsicles 43
21. Blueberry Fat Bombs 45

22. Cream Cheese Fat Bombs ... 47
23. Chocolate Macadamia Fat Bomb ... 49
24. Happy Almond Bombs ... 51
25. Blackberry Coconut Fat Bombs ... 53
26. Ginger Fat Bombs ... 55
27. Lemon Clouds ... 57
28. Orange Pecan Butter Fat Bombs ... 59
29. Cheesy Pesto Fat Bombs ... 61
30. Cream Cheese and Peanut Butter Fat Bomb ... 63
31. Chocolate Mousse ... 65
32. Chocolate Fat Bombs ... 67
33. Peanut Butter Fudge ... 69
34. Buttered Bacon Fat Bomb ... 71
35. Mocha Vanilla Fat Bomb Pops ... 73
Part 2 ... 75
Introduction ... 76
Chapter 1: The Basics and Benefits of the Keto Diet ... 78
Chapter 2: All about Fat Bombs ... 86
Chapter 3: Sweet Fat Bomb Recipes ... 98
Almond Coconut Fat Bomb ... 98
Carrot Cake Fat Bomb ... 101
Chai Fat Bomb ... 103
Chocolate Brownie Fat Bomb ... 105
Chocolate Cherry Fat Bomb ... 107
Chocolate Coconut Oil Fat Bomb ... 109
Chocolate Fat Bomb ... 111
Creamed Blueberry Fat Bomb ... 113

Danish Butter Cookie Fat Bomb 115
Ginger Fat Bomb 117
Hazelnut Fat Bomb 119
Mocha Peppermint Fat Bomb 122
Orange Fat Bomb 125
Peanut Butter Fat Bomb 127
Peppermint Andes Fat Bomb 129
Red Velvet Fat Bomb 131
Chapter 4: Savory Fat Bomb Recipes 134
Alfredo Fat Bomb 134
Avocado & Ham Fat Bomb 136
Barbeque Chicken Fat Bomb 138
Buttery Bacon Fat Bomb 141
Cauliflower Cheese Fat Bomb 144
Cheeseburger Fat Bomb 148
Cream Cheese Fat Bomb 150
Pistachio Fat Bomb 152
Pizza Fat Bomb 154
Sausage & Cheese Fat Bomb 156
Spicy Bacon & Cheese Fat Bomb 159
Chapter 5: Frozen Fat Bomb Recipes 162
Butter Cream Fat Bomb 162
Butter Pecan Fat Bomb 165
Caramel Peanut Butter Fat Bomb 168
Cheesecake Fat Bomb 170
Chocolate Chip Cookie Dough Fat Bomb 172
Chocolate Sea Salt Fat Bomb 174

Cookies & Cream Fat Bomb 176
Creamsickle Fat Bomb 179
Iced Coffee Fat Bomb 181
Mint Chocolate Chip Fat Bomb 183
Peanut Butter Whip Fat Bomb 185
Pumpkin Fat Bomb 188
Rocky Road Fat Bomb 190
Conclusion 192

Part 1

INTRODUCTION

What Are Ketogenic Fat Bombs?

Many people are paranoid when it comes to eating fat. Although it has been public enemy number one for a long time, research has confirmed that fats can be extremely healthy. The only condition you need to fulfill is to choose the right type of fats. According to scientific reports, saturated fats, found in butter, coconut oil, cream cheese, and heavy cream influence our levels of good cholesterol. Proper levels good cholesterol improves our chances of avoiding and fighting heart disease, decreases our blood pressure, enhances our overall health, and, last but not least, gets our weight in order.

What a fat bomb contains.

1. Fat bombs are either sweet or savory. You'll find more recipes that swing towards the sweet side, but there are plenty savory recipe options available. A lot the sweeter recipes call for stevia, a low-calorie and no-carb sweetener. Many savory fat bombs are made with items like bacon, chicken, sausage, or salmon.
2. Fat bombs are small. These items are high in fat so, they are meant to be eaten in small servings. They

will normally take the shape miniature muffins or a small ball.
3. Fat bombs can be made in large batches then stored in the refrigerator or freezer. Many fat bomb recipes make 10 or more servings at a time. They are ideal for people who want to cook once or twice a week and have healthy options on hand throughout the week. Fat bombs contain a high amount of fat and therefore will need to be kept cold when stored. These items are not meant to sit at room temperature for long periods. Fat bombs usually last for between 1 and 2 weeks when properly stored.
4. Fat bombs are high in healthy fats. These healthy fats are important when following a keto diet because they help lower levels inflammation in the body. Many keto fat bombs will have some form of coconut butter or coconut oil in them. These oils help solidify the fat bombs and make them less a mess to eat.
5. Fat bombs will often have seeds or nuts. Nuts are only meant to be eaten in small amounts due to the number carbohydrates they contain. This makes them ideal for fat bombs. Peanuts are not technically nuts, so the keto diet substitutes peanut butter with almond butter in their recipes.

Why Do You Need Ketogenic Fat Bombs?

As I mentioned, there are some fats that are bad, and these are called trans fats. On the other hand, there are 'good fats' that you should eat to help dissolve different vitamins, such as vitamins A, D, E, and K. Fat bombs also help reduce our bad cholesterol levels (LDL) and improve the amount good cholesterol (HDL).

Those you who are aiming to get rid extra pounds will surely be delighted to hear that fat bombs can help us get our weight under control. Each these recipes perfectly fits into ketogenic diet plans. Naturally, you will need to track your portion sizes; in other words, you can't eat too many these fat bombs.

Now that we are familiar with what fat bombs are let's move on to the recipes. I have included several recipes rich in healthy fats which also fit perfectly with a ketogenic diet.

Chapter 1: 14 Useful drinks you should know

1. Smoothie

Serving: 1 fat bomb

Prep Time: 5 min

Ingredients

- 1/2 teaspoon and 1/8 teaspoon cinnamon, divided
- 6 drops liquid stevia
- 6 ice cubes
- 6 ounces half-and-half
- 1 tablespoon softened cream cheese
- 1 teaspoon vanilla extract

Instructions

- Add the half-and-half and cream cheese to a blender to combine.
- Add 1/2 teaspoon cinnamon, vanilla, and stevia then blend for 1 minute or until well mixed.
- Pour the ice cubes in and blend until the smoothie thickens.
- Sprinkle 1/8 teaspoon cinnamon on top and serve.

Nutrients per one serving: Calories: 283, Fat: 24g, Protein: 6g, Sodium: 116mg, Fiber: 1g, Carbohydrates: 9g, Sugar: 1g

2. Po Cha

Serving: 2 people

Prep Time: 3 min

Cook Time: 8 min

Ingredients

- 2 tablespoons heavy cream
- 1/8 teaspoon sea salt
- 1 drop smoke flavor
- 4 cups water
- 2 tablespoons black tea leaves
- 2 tablespoons butter

Instructions

- Bring some water to a boil in a small saucepan then lower the heat to low.
- Add some tea leaves to the water and simmer for about 3 minutes, then strain.
- Combine the brewed tea with the remaining ingredients in a blender, then mix on high for about 3 minutes.
- Serve immediately.

Nutrients per one serving: Calories: 153, Fat: 17g, Protein: 0g, Sodium: 169mg, Fiber: 0g, Carbohydrates: 0g, Sugar: 0g

3. Creamy Coconut Smoothie

Serving: 1 fat bomb

Prep Time: 5 min

Ingredients

- 1/2 (13.5-ounce) can coconut milk
- 1 tablespoon unsweetened shredded coconut
- 6 drops liquid stevia
- 1 tablespoon powdered unflavored gelatin
- 1 tablespoon softened coconut oil
- 1 teaspoon vanilla extract

- 6 ice cubes

Instructions

- Pour the milk and gelatin into a blender then blend until combined.
- Add everything except for the ice cubes and blend for 1 minute or until well mixed.
- Pour the ice cubes in and blend until the smoothie thickens.
- Serve immediately.

Nutrients per one serving: Calories: 559, Fat: 57g, Protein: 10g, Sodium: 41mg, Fiber: 0g, Carbohydrates: 7g, Sugar: 1g

4. Creamy Mexican Hot Chocolate

Serving: 2 people

Prep Time: 3 min

Cook Time: 5 min

Ingredients

- 1/8 teaspoon vanilla extract
- 1 cup water
- 1 cup heavy cream
- 2 teaspoons erythritol or granular Swerve, or 2 drops stevia glycerite
- 4 tablespoons unsweetened whipped cream
- 1/3 cup cocoa powder

- 1 teaspoon cinnamon

Instructions

- Combine all the ingredients except the whipped cream in a saucepan over very low heat.
- Stir frequently while heating until the cocoa powder is completely dissolved, about 5 minutes. Avoid boiling.
- When it's ready to serve, pour into 2 cups then top with whipped cream.

Nutrients per one serving: Calories: 538, Fat: 56g, Protein: 6g, Sodium: 63mg, Fiber: 5g, Carbohydrates: 17g, Sugar: 0g

5. Eggnog Smoothie

Serving: 2 fat bombs

Prep Time: 10 min

Ingredients

- 2 large eggs, the yolk and white separated
- 8 ounces heavy cream
- 8 drops liquid stevia
- 1 tablespoon granular Swerve
- 8 ice cubes

- 1/2 teaspoon vanilla extract
- 1 teaspoon nutmeg
- 1/8 teaspoon ground cloves
- 3/8 teaspoon cinnamon, divided

Instructions

- In a medium bowl, beat the egg whites using a hand mixer until stiff peaks form. Keep aside.
- In a separate large bowl, beat the yolks using a mixer until the color changes to pale yellow.
- Add vanilla, nutmeg, cream, cloves, 1/8 teaspoon cinnamon, stevia, and Swerve then stir well to combine.
- Fold the whites into the yolk mixture.
- Pour the mix into a blender with the ice cubes, then blend until the mixture thickens.
- Sprinkle 1/8 teaspoon cinnamon on the top every glass then serve immediately.

Nutrients per one serving: Calories: 468, Fat: 47g, Protein: 9g, Sodium: 113mg, Fiber: 1g, Carbohydrates: 5g, Sugar: 1g

6. Gingerbread Gem Smoothie

Serving: 1 fat bomb

Prep Time: 5 min

Ingredients

- 1/2 teaspoon ground ginger
- 1/2 teaspoon cinnamon
- 6 drops liquid stevia
- 6 ice cubes

- 6 ounces unsweetened almond milk
- 1 tablespoon powdered unflavored gelatin
- 1 tablespoon almond butter
- 1/2 teaspoon vanilla extract

Instructions

- Pour the milk and gelatin into a blender then blend until combined.
- Add everything except for the ice cubes and blend for 1 minute or until well mixed.
- Pour the ice cubes in and blend until the smoothie thickens.
- Serve immediately.

Nutrients per one serving: Calories: 221, Fat: 11g, Protein: 16g, Sodium: 174mg, Fiber: 3g, Carbohydrates: 16g, Sugar: 9g

7. Key Lime Pie Smoothie

Serving: 1 fat bomb

Prep Time: 5 min

Ingredients

- 1 teaspoon lime zest
- 6 drops liquid stevia
- 6 ice cubes
- 6 ounces half-and-half
- 1 tablespoon powdered unflavored gelatin
- 1 teaspoon vanilla extract
- 2 tablespoons freshly squeezed key lime juice

Instructions

- Pour the half-and-half and gelatin into a blender then blend until combined.
- Add everything except for the ice cubes and blend for 1 minute or until well mixed.
- Pour the ice cubes in and blend until the smoothie thickens.
- Serve immediately.

Nutrients per one serving: Calories: 280, Fat: 20g, Protein: 12g, Sodium: 91mg, Fiber: 2g, Carbohydrates: 17g, Sugar: 3g

8. Matcha Madness Smoothie

Serving: 1 fat bomb

Prep Time: 5 min

Ingredients

- 1/2 (13.5-ounce) can coconut milk
- 1 tablespoon matcha
- 6 drops liquid stevia
- Ice cubes
- 1 tablespoon powdered unflavored gelatin
- 2 tablespoons almond butter

- 1 teaspoon vanilla extract

Instructions

- Pour milk and gelatin into a blender then blend until combined.
- Add everything except for the ice cubes and blend for 1 minute or until well mixed.
- Pour the ice cubes in and blend until the smoothie thickens.
- Serve immediately.

Nutrients per one serving: Calories: 610, Fat: 57g, Protein: 19g, Sodium: 187mg, Fiber: 4g, Carbohydrates: 15g, Sugar: 4g

9. Peanut Butter Cup Smoothie

Serving: 1 fat bomb

Prep Time: 5 min

Ingredients

- 2 tablespoons cocoa powder
- 1 teaspoon vanilla extract
- 6 drops liquid stevia
- Ice cubes
- 1/2 (13.5-ounce) can coconut milk
- 1 tablespoon powdered unflavored gelatin
- 2 tablespoons peanut butter

Instructions

- Pour the milk and gelatin into a blender then blend until combined.
- Add everything except for the ice cubes and blend for 1 minute or until well mixed.
- Pour the ice cubes in and blend until the smoothie thickens.
- Serve immediately.

Nutrients per one serving: Calories: 622, Fat: 58g, Protein: 20g, Sodium: 189mg, Fiber: 6g, Carbohydrates: 18g, Sugar: 4g

10. Amaretto Chilled Coffee

Serving: 2 fat bombs

Prep Time: 8 min

Ingredients

- 2 cups cooled brewed coffee
- 1/2 cup chilled heavy cream
- 1 teaspoon crumbled roasted almonds

- 4 teaspoons erythritol or granular Swerve /3 drops stevia glycerite, divided
- 4 drops divided amaretto flavor

Instructions

- Pour coffee into a medium bowl then add half the sweetener and half the amaretto flavor and mix.
- In a blender, add the chilled cream, the remaining amaretto flavor, and the remaining sweetener, then blend on high until the cream is whipped.
- Once it is ready to serve, pour the coffee mixture over the ice in 2 glasses.
- Spoon the whipped cream on top of the coffee mix. Decorate using chopped almonds.
- Serve immediately using a spoon and straw.

Nutrients per one serving: Calories: 421, Fat: 23g, Protein: 12g, Sodium: 55mg, Fiber: 0g, Carbohydrates: 45g, Sugar: 0g

11. Vanilla Smoothie

Serving: 1 fat bomb

Prep Time: 5 min

Ingredients

- The pulp of 1 vanilla bean, scraped
- 4 drops liquid stevia
- 6 ice cubes
- 6 ounces half-and-half
- 1 tablespoon powdered unflavored gelatin

- 1 teaspoon vanilla extract

Instructions

- Pour the half-and-half and gelatin into a blender then blend until combined.
- Add everything except for the ice cubes and blend for 1 minute or until well mixed.
- Pour the ice cubes in and blend until the smoothie thickens.
- Serve immediately.

Nutrients per one serving: Calories: 274, Fat: 19g, Protein: 11g, Sodium: 83mg, Fiber: 0g, Carbohydrates: 8g, Sugar: 1g

12. Vanilla Avocado Smoothie

Serving: 1 fat bomb
Prep Time: 5 min

Ingredients

- 1/2 (13.5-ounce) can coconut milk
- 1 teaspoon vanilla extract
- 6 drops liquid stevia
- 4 ice cubes
- 1 tablespoon powdered unflavored gelatin
- 1 tablespoon ground flaxseed

- 1/2 pitted and peeled medium avocado

Instructions

- Pour gelatin, milk, and flaxseed into a blender then blend until combined.
- Add everything except for the ice cubes and blend for 1 minute or until well mixed.
- Pour the ice cubes in and blend until the smoothie thickens.
- Serve immediately.

Nutrients per one serving: Calories: 603, Fat: 57g, Protein: 14g, Sodium: 46mg, Fiber: 9g, Carbohydrates: 17g, Sugar: 1g

13. Vanilla Almond Butter Smoothie

Serving: 1 fat bomb

Prep Time: 5 min

Ingredients

- 6 ounces unsweetened almond milk
- 1/4 teaspoon almond extract (optional)
- 6 drops liquid stevia
- 6 ice cubes
- 1 tablespoon powdered unflavored gelatin
- 2 tablespoons almond butter

- 1 teaspoon vanilla extract

Instructions

- Pour the milk and gelatin into a blender then blend until combined.
- Add everything except for the ice cubes and blend for 1 minute or until well mixed.
- Pour the ice cubes in and blend until the smoothie thickens.
- Serve immediately.

Nutrients per one serving: Calories: 316, Fat: 19g, Protein: 19g, Sodium: 248mg, Fiber: 3g, Carbohydrates: 17g, Sugar: 10g

14. Strawberry Vanilla Smoothie

Serving: 1 fat bomb

Prep Time: 5 min

Ingredients

- 1/2 (13.5-ounce) can coconut milk
- 1/4 cup chopped fresh strawberries
- 6 drops liquid stevia
- 1 tablespoon powdered unflavored gelatin
- 1 tablespoon softened coconut oil
- 1 teaspoon vanilla extract

- 6 ice cubes

Instructions

- Pour the milk and gelatin into a blender then blend until combined.
- Add everything except for the ice cubes and blend for 1 minute or until well mixed.
- Pour the ice cubes in and blend until the smoothie thickens.
- Serve immediately.

Nutrients per one serving: Calories: 540, Fat: 54g, Protein: 10g, Sodium: 39mg, Fiber: 1g, Carbohydrates: 9g, Sugar: 2g

Chapter 2: How to have a delicious dish quickly and easily

15. Salted Caramel Almond

Serving: 12 fat bombs

Prep Time: 3 hours

Cook Time: 5 minutes

Ingredients

- 1/4 cup granular Swerve

- 2 teaspoons vanilla extract
- 12 whole almonds
- 1/4 cup butter
- 1 teaspoon coarse sea salt

Instructions

- Combine Swerve, butter, and vanilla in a small saucepan over medium heat. Stir frequently until the ingredients melt. Turn off heat.
- Place 1 almond in each mold of a 12-mold silicone candy tray.
- Add the mixture until the molds become about 3/4 full.
- Sprinkle salt on top of every fat bomb.
- Freeze until set, then serve from the freezer.

Nutrients per one serving: Calories: 64, Fat: 7g, Protein: 0g, Sodium: 296mg, Fiber: 0g, Carbohydrates: 1g, Sugar: 0g

16. Mocha Ice Bombs

Serving: 12 people

Prep Time: 10 min

Ingredients

- 1/4cup powdered sweetener
- 2 tbsp. unsweetened cocoa
- 1/4cup strong coffee chilled
- 1cup cream cheese

Chocolate coating

- 70g melted chocolate
- 28g melted cocoa butter

Instructions

- Add coffee to the cream cheese, cocoa, and sweetener.
- Blend until smooth.
- To make an ice bomb shape, roll 2 tablespoons of the mocha ice bomb mixture to a ball, then place on a tray or plate lined with baking parchment.
- Chocolate coating
- Mix the melted chocolate and cocoa butter together.
- Roll every ice bomb in chocolate coating then place back on the lined tray/plate.
- Place in a freezer for about 2 hours.

Nutrients per one serving: Calories 127, Total fat 12.9g, Total Carbs 2.2g, Protein 1.9g

17. Low Carb Frozen Chocolate Chip Balls

Serving: 16 people

Prep Time: 10 min

Ingredients

- 1/4 cup cocoa powder, unsweetened
- 1/2 cup Splenda (granulated)
- 1/2 cup low carb chocolate chips
- 1/4 cup water
- 1 Brick cream cheese

- 1 stick unsalted butter

Instructions

- Mix the cocoa powder and water until a thick paste is formed.
- Add the cream cheese, butter, cocoa mixture, and Splenda to a stand mixer then mix until smooth.
- Stir in chocolate chips.
- Form the mixture into 16 1" diameter balls. Put on a tray or pan lined with a silicone mat or baking parchment.
- Freeze for 1 hour then transfer to a lidded container.
- Remove from freezer about 10 minutes before eating.

Nutrients per one serving: Total carbs 5.7g, Fiber 06g, Protein 3.6g, Fat 34.6g, Magnesium 15mg, Potassium 94mg

18. Valentine's Day Keto Fat Bombs

Serving: 4 people

Prep time:2 min

Cook time:2 min

Ingredients

- 1 teaspoon Cocoa Powder
- 2 Oz Dark Chocolate
- 8 Drops EZ-Sweetz
- 2 Oz. Almond Butter
- 2 Oz. Coconut Oil
- 1 Oz. Cream Cheese
- ½ Oz. Torani Sugar-Free Vanilla Syrup

Instructions

- Combine all items except the almond butter and microwave for about 30 seconds on high
- Stir the ingredients and microwave again. Repeat until the chocolate melts.
- Pour the base layer into the mold you are using
- Then use a spoon to dollop Almond Butter in the center of each mold.
- Fill the mold to the top with the chocolate mix
- Freeze until the chocolate becomes hard, then hard push these out of the mold
- Store in a fridge

Nutrients per one serving: Calories 297, Fat 30, Carbs 7, Fiber 3, Protein 5

19. Ice Cream

Serving: 5 people

Prep Time: 10 min

Ingredients
- 1/3 cup xylitol
- 1/3 cup flavor variation
- ¼ cup MCT oil
- 4 pastured eggs, whole
- 4 pastured eggs yolks
- 1/3 cup melted cacao butter
- 1/3 cup melted coconut oil
- 2 tsp vanilla bean powder

- 8-10 ice cubes

Instructions

- Add everything except the ice cubes to a high powered blender. Blend on high for about 2 minutes, or until creamy.
- As the blender runs, remove the top portion of the lid and drop in the ice cubes, one at a time, allowing the blender to run for about 10 seconds between every ice cube.
- Once you have added all the ice, pour the cold mixture into an ice cream maker and churn it on high for about 20-30 minutes, as per the ice cream maker directions.
- Serve this immediately as a soft-serve or scoop it into 9 * 5 loaf pan and freeze for about 45 minutes. Store while covered in freezer for about a week.

Nutrients per one serving: Calories: 431, Calories from Fat: 399, Saturated Fat: 34 g, Total Fat: 44.3, Sodium: 56 mg, Carbs: 3.4 g, Cholesterol: 299> mg, Dietary Fiber: 1.6 g, Protein: 7.7 g, Net Carbs: 1.8 g

20. Blueberry Cheesecake Popsicles

Serving: 10 people

Prep Time: 5 minutes

Ingredients

- 8 Tbsps. light cream cheese
- 6 Tbsps. icing sugar
- 2 cups fresh blueberries
- 30 Tbsps. Cool Whip

Instructions

- Puree the blueberries, cream cheese, and icing sugar in a blender until smooth.
- Gently fold in the whipped topping.
- Spoon into popsicle molds then freeze until firm.
- Run the mold under hot water to loosen the popsicles so they are easy to release.

Nutrients per one serving: 83 calories, 3 fat, 1 protein, 15 carbs.

21. Blueberry Fat Bombs

Serving: 24 fat bombs

Prep Time: 10 min

Ingredients

- 1 stick butter (4 oz.)
- Scant cup blueberries
- 3/4 c. coconut oil
- 4 oz. softened cream cheese
- ¼ c. coconut cream
- Sweetener to taste

Instructions

- In a food processor, place the coconut cream, berries, and soft cream cheese.
- Puree until smooth.
- In a saucepan over low heat, melt the coconut oil and butter.
- Let cool for about 5 minutes, then add to the food processor and puree again until smooth.
- Slowly, add the sweetener of your choice while tasting and adjusting to your liking.
- Transfer the mixture into molds leaving space at the top.
- Freeze for one hour and enjoy.
- You can also freeze them in suitable plastic bags.

Nutrients per one serving: 116 calories, 44gprotein, 13gfat, 1.02gcarbs 84g NET CARBS, .18gfiber

22. Cream Cheese Fat Bombs

Serving: 2 balls

Prep Time: 10 minutes

Cook Time: 5 minutes

Ingredients

- Sugar-free Jell-O, 1 package, or pudding mix
- 1 8oz package Kraft Philadelphia cream cheese

Instructions

- Cut the cream cheese into 16 squares.
- Put the Jell-O or pudding mix into a small bowl.

- Cover each cream cheese square on all the sides using the mix.
- Roll into a ball.
- Keep covered with a plastic wrap inside your fridge.

Nutrients per one serving: 105 calories, 9 g fat, 1 carb, and 3 g protein

23. Chocolate Macadamia Fat Bomb

Serving: 6 people

Prep Time: 5 minutes

Cook Time: 5 minutes

Ingredients

- 4 oz. Chopped macadamias
- ¼ cup Heavy cream or coconut oil
- 2 oz. Cocoa Butter

- 2 Tbs unsweetened cocoa powder
- 2 Tbs Swerve

Instructions

- Melt the cocoa butter in a small saucepan.
- Add cocoa powder and Swerve then mix well.
- Add the macadamias then stir in well.
- Add cream, then mix well, bring it back to temperature.
- Pour in molds or paper candy cups.
- Allow to cool, then place in a fridge to harden.
- Store at room temperature.

Nutrients per one serving: Calories 267, Fat 28gm, Net carbs 3gm, Protein 3gm

24. Happy Almond Bombs

Serving: 4 people

Prep Time: 5 minutes

Cook Time: 5 minutes

Ingredients

- 4 tablespoons almond butter
- 1oz cream cheese
- 4 tablespoons coconut butter
- 1 tablespoon cocoa powder
- 2 tablespoons sugar-free syrup
- 16g dark chocolate

Instructions

- Add everything except the coconut butter in a microwave-safe dish.
- Microwave in 15 seconds intervals, stirring every time, until the chocolate and cream cheese have melted and all ingredients have fully incorporated.
- Add coconut butter and mix.
- Spoon the batter into 12 portions in a mini-muffin tray.
- Pop these into a freezer for about 1 hour to set. Enjoy.

Nutrients per one serving: Calories 86, Total fat 7g, Total carbs 3g, protein 2g, cholesterol 3mg, sodium 21mg

25. Blackberry Coconut Fat Bombs

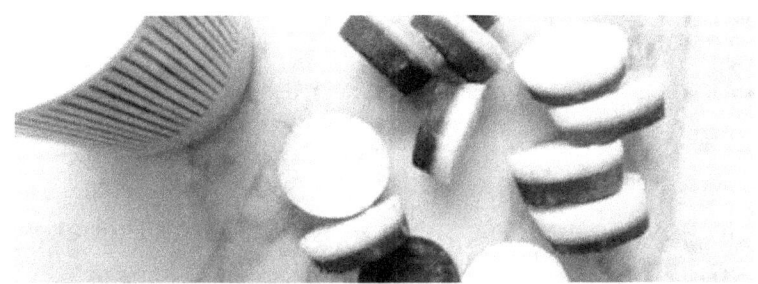

Serving: 6 people

Total Time: 10 minutes

Ingredients

- 1 cup coconut butter
- 1/2 cup frozen blackberries can
- 1/2 teaspoon Sweat leaf Stevia drops
- 1/4 teaspoon vanilla powder or a 1/2 teaspoon vanilla extract
- 1 tablespoon lemon juice
- 1 cup coconut oil

Instructions

- Place the coconut oil, coconut butter, and blackberries in a pot then heat over medium heat until well combined.
- In a food processor or small blender, add the berry mix and the remaining ingredients. Mix until smooth.
- Spread out on a small pan lined with a parchment paper
- Refrigerate for one hour.
- Remove from the container then cut into squares.
- Store while covered in a refrigerator.

Nutrients per one serving: Calories 170Calories from Fat 168, Total Fat 18.7g, Total carbohydrates 3g, Dietary Fiber 2.3g, Protein 1.1g

26. Ginger Fat Bombs

Serving: 10 people

Prep Time: 10 min

Ingredients

- 75g / 2.6oz coconut butter
- 75g / 2.6oz coconut oil
- 25g / 1oz shredded/desiccated coconut
- 1 tsp granulated sweetener
- 1/2-1 tsp ginger powder

Instructions

- Mix all the ingredients in a pouring jug until the sweetener dissolves.
- Pour into silicon molds or ice block trays then refrigerate for around 10 minutes.

Nutrients per one serving: Calories 120, Total Fat 12.8g, Fiber 1.4g, Sugars 0.1g, Protein 0.5g

27. Lemon Clouds

Serving: 16 bombs

Prep Time: 10 min

Ingredients

- 1 lemon, squeezed
- 1 tsp lemon extract
- Sweetener to taste
- Silicone mold or ice cube tray
- 4 tbsps. butter
- 4 tbsps. virgin coconut oil
- 2oz cream cheese
- 4 tbsps. heavy cream

Instructions

- Begin with the cream cheese, heating it in short bursts.
- Add the butter and coconut oil, then whisk until well blended.
- Add the cream last then whisk.
- Squeeze in the lemon, watching for the pesky seeds. Add extract if needed.
- Sweeten to taste.
- Carefully pour into the tray then balance in the freezer overnight.
- Pop them from the tray in the next morning.

Nutrients per one serving: Calories: 74.7, Fat: 8g, Protein: 0.3g, Carbs: 0.7g, Fiber: 0.8g, Sugars: 0.3g

28. Orange Pecan Butter Fat Bombs

Serving: 2 people

Prep Time: 10 min

Ingredients

- 4 pecan halves
- 1/2 tbsp. unsalted grass-fed butter
- 1/2 tsp orange zest, finely grated
- 1 pinch sea salt

Instructions

- Toast the pecans at 350° in an oven for 8-10 minutes, then keep aside to cool.
- Soften butter, then add orange zest and mix well until smooth and creamy.
- Spread half the butter-orange mixture in two pecan halves. Sprinkle using sea salt then enjoy.

Nutrients per one serving: Calories 89, Net carbs 1

29. Cheesy Pesto Fat Bombs

Serving: 8 people

Prep Time: 5 min

Ingredients

- 10 sliced olives
- Salt, pepper to taste (optional)
- 1 cup full-fat cream cheese
- 2 tbsps. basil pesto
- ½ cup grated Parmesan cheese

Instructions

- Place all ingredients in a bowl using a spatula until well combined.
- Slice a cucumber or the other fresh vegetable which you are planning to serve it with.
- Place remaining dip in an airtight container in a fridge for a week.

Nutrients per one serving: Total Carbs 1.6g, Fiber 0.3g, Protein 4.3g, Fat 12.9g, Magnesium 37mg, Potassium 50mg

30. Cream Cheese and Peanut Butter Fat Bomb

Serving: 14 pieces

Prep Time: 10 min

Ingredients

- 2 Tablespoons sour cream
- 4 Tablespoons softened cream cheese
- 1 cup heavy whipping cream
- 3 Tablespoons BP2 peanut butter, powdered
- 2 Tablespoons Splenda

Instructions

- Whip heavy whipping cream until it is light and airy.
- Add the remaining ingredients and mix well.
- Spoon into a silicone candy mold tray to make 14 portions, then freeze overnight.
- Serve them partially frozen or allow them to defrost completely for a fluffy treat.

Nutrients per one serving: Calories 82, Total fat 8g, Cholesterol 24mg, Sodium 29mg, Totals carbs 1g, Protein 1g

31. Chocolate Mousse

Serving: 4 people

Prep Time: 5 min

Ingredients

- ½ tsp cinnamon
- 6-12 drops liquid stevia extract
- Shredded coconut for garnish
- 1 cup creamed coconut milk
- 3 tbsps. raw cocoa powder

Instructions

- Put the can of coconut milk in the fridge overnight. Once thick, pour into a bowl.
- Whip in raw cocoa powder.
- Add in cinnamon and stevia.
- Whip until smooth and creamy.
- Place in serving glasses, then garnish using a pinch of shredded coconut. Enjoy!

Nutrients per one serving: Total Carbs 13.5g, Fiber 5.8g, Protein 6.2g, Fat 42.9g, Magnesium 75mg, Potassium 520mg

32. Chocolate Fat Bombs

Serving: 14 people

Prep Time: 10 min

Ingredients

- 125g / 4.5oz coconut oil
- 25g / 1oz unsweetened cocoa powder
- 1 tbsp. granulated sweetener
- 1-2 tbsps. tahini paste
- 25g / 1oz walnut halves

Instructions

- Warm the coconut oil until it melts.

- Add everything except the walnuts and allow to cool so the ingredients do not settle and sink to the bottom your fat bomb.
- Pour into ice cube trays then refrigerate until it is semi-set.
- Once it's almost set, put half a walnut on top of every fat bomb.

Nutrients per one serving: Calories 119, Total fat 12.6g, Total Carbs 1.2g, Protein 1.4g

33. Peanut Butter Fudge

Serving: 12 people

Prep Time: 5 min

Ingredients

- 1 cup unsweetened peanut butter
- 1/4 cup unsweetened cocoa powder
- 1 cup coconut oil
- 1/4 cup vanilla almond milk, unsweetened
- Pinch salt (optional)
- 2 teaspoons vanilla liquid stevia (optional)
- 2 tablespoons coconut oil, melted
- 2 tablespoons Swerve

Instructions

- Slightly melt/soften the peanut butter and coconut oil in the microwave or over low heat on a stove.
- Add the mix and remaining ingredients to a blender.
- Blend until well combined.
- Pour into a loaf pan with lined with parchment paper.
- Refrigerate for 2 hours until set.
- If you are using chocolate sauce, whisk the ingredients together then drizzle over the fudge after it has set.

Nutrients per one serving: Calories 287, Fat29.7g, Carbs 4g, Sugar 0.7g, Sodium 4mg, Fiber 1.4g, Protein 5.4g

34. Buttered Bacon Fat Bomb

Serving: 3 fat bombs

Prep Time: 2 min

Ingredients

- 1 bacon slice
- 2 toasted & chopped pecan halves
- 1/16 serving Keto Craisin
- 1 tablespoon unsalted Kerrygold butter
- 1 pinch granulated garlic (optional)

Instructions

- Divide your bacon into 3 parts. Slather each using 1 teaspoon of Kerrygold unsalted butter.
- Press the butter side into your pecan pieces.
- Top each using Keto Craisin.

Nutrients per one serving: 158 Calories, 2g Protein, 17g Fat, 1g Carbohydrate, 1g Effective Carbs, trace Dietary Fiber

35. Mocha Vanilla Fat Bomb Pops

Serving: 6 people

Prep Time: 10 min

Ingredients
- 2 tbsps. heavy cream
- 1/2 tsp vanilla extract
- 4 tbsps. coconut oil
- 1/2 tbsp. unsweetened cocoa powder
- 4 tbsps. unsalted butter
- 1/2 tsp coffee extract
- Stevia, to taste

Instructions

Make vanilla layer:

- Soften butter in a microwave until liquefied.
- Add the heavy cream and stir. Keep aside.
- Once cooled, add vanilla, then blend well.
- Pour vanilla mixture into muffin liners/tins. Place into refrigerator until firm.

Make mocha layer:

- Mix coconut oil, coffee extract, cocoa powder, and stevia.
- Remove the vanilla layer from the fridge, then pour in mocha mixture, filling the cups to the top.
- Add popsicle sticks then freeze for 20 to 30 minutes.

Nutrition information per serving: 167 Calories; trace Protein, 19g Fat, .5g Dietary Fiber, 1g Carbohydrate

Part 2

Introduction

Whether you are new to the Keto diet or have been testing out the dishes for years, you will find the fat bomb recipes, baking, and recipe variation tips will help you prepare a healthy variety of fat bombs that will make your mouth water. The plan goes by many different names such as the low-carb diet, the Keto diet, and the low-carbohydrate diet & high fat (LCHF) diet plan. However, we will keep it simple and call it the Keto diet in this cookbook.

The recipes in this book are easy to make, and many do not take that much time out of your day as we know that time is most important to everybody. There is also an overview as to how to follow the diet and how to integrate the Keto diet easily into your life. Many of these recipes take you less than half an hour and can be eaten right away or stored for that afternoon snack you crave.

The recipes that you will find inside will not only satisfy your rumbling stomach, but it will also make you feel good that you are taking this step towards a healthier life. We hope that this cookbook helps to show you the world of possibilities with the Keto diet.

A few of the recipes may require a few more steps, but each recipe will provide you with a short description, an estimated preparation and cooking time, amount of servings, and a list of nutritional values including calories, net carbohydrates, protein, sugar, and fats. It is all laid out for you in a simple-to-follow list of instructions to get started on the Keto diet today.

There are plenty of books on the Keto diet in the market today. Thanks again for choosing this one! Every effort was made to ensure that it is full of as much useful information as possible.

Chapter 1: The Basics and Benefits of the Keto Diet

If you are just getting started, there is a lot of information to take in. However, this mini-guide will ease the pressure a bit and give you some direction. Let us get started!

The Basics of the Keto Diet

The word Keto comes from the term "Ketogenic", which is a medical expression that defines the state of the body when ketones are produced from fat consumption. Your body ordinarily produces glucose from carbohydrate intake which is where the body gets its source of energy. However, if carb ingestion is too high, it will result in weight gain and health complications.

For example, the standard American diet contains approximately 60% of carbs. Compare this to the Keto diet where you will be consuming about 75% healthy fats and keep carb intake around 5%. When you make this switch in your diet, you will generally see the weight loss benefits due to your body producing the ketones, which is exactly the goal of the Keto diet.

As with any change in lifestyle, consult your doctor about your specific needs as the Keto diet is not for everyone.

What are Ketones?

Ketones are a very important chemical in the Keto diet because it is the ultimate goal for your liver to create these ketones, which is the result of fat in your body being recycled for fuel. This process occurs when there is a deficit of insulin in your body. The insulin is responsible for transferring the glucose or sugars into the energy you need every day to function properly.

What is Ketosis?

Most of the information that has been studied about Ketosis is for people who have fasted. This is due to the process of Ketosis starting when the body has expended the carbs present, which in turn makes the liver start creating ketones to make up the deficit. When you fast for longer than 72 hours, the liver will create even more ketones.

Now, you are not going to be fasting by a long shot. You are going to be transforming your relationship with food so that you can easily reach your goals without feeling hungry. The Keto diet keeps your carb intake low so that it tricks your body that you are essentially fasting, which keeps your liver to produce the ketones needed for your body to stay in Ketosis.

There is a balance with how many macronutrients you consume to keep the level of Ketosis you desire in your body on the Keto diet. If you, for example, eat too many proteins, your insulin levels will rise. As we learned, this will take your body out of Ketosis. As a result, the insulin will create the sugars that your body is used to using for fuel and stops the production of ketones by the liver.

The Benefits of the Keto Diet

Several benefits affect people differently. The main advantage that most people will notice is weight loss, and conclusions from several medical studies state it is a healthy way of doing so. The reasoning for this is most of the weight lost is water weight due to the carbs being expended in the liver.
Most people see the results quickly which keeps them motivated to keep going towards their personal goals.

Another benefit that you may experience is you will not be snacking throughout the day. This is due to the high amount of fats that are present in the Keto diet, and these fats are a potent source of energy for your body.

Your body is left more satisfied, and in return, you will see your energy levels soar and be able to keep you more focused throughout the day. This also reduces the sugar crashes experienced prior because sugar consumption is eliminated.

The other main benefit that followers will experience is a leveling out of the blood sugar levels. When you are not fueling your body with carbs, this naturally lowers the blood sugars. This is why people with Type 2 diabetes decide to follow this diet along with the weight loss factor.

This diet can also benefit children who experience epileptic seizures and can also be beneficial to adults who suffer from the same. As stated above, it is best to talk with your health care professional as the Keto diet may complicate some medications and health issues.

Guidelines on What Foods to Eat

Here is an easy to follow list of what is allowed on the Keto diet.

- Eggs: This is the most versatile item on the list because you can have eggs in any form that you wish.
- Vegetables: Generally, you will stick to the ones that grow above the ground.

- Seafood and fish: These are an excellent source of fats.
- Meat: Stick to the unprocessed cuts to keep true to the diet.
- Dairy: The items that are high in fats such as butter and cheese.
- Berries: The best ones to have in your diet are blackberries, blueberries, raspberries, and strawberries.
- Nuts: The most popular are almond, pecans, macadamia, and walnuts.
- Drinks: Coffee and Tea can be consumed without sugar and of course water.

What Foods Not to Eat

- Milk: The sugars contained in milk makes it very high in carbs.
- Whole Fruits: Bananas, oranges, apples, and peaches. This includes dried fruits as they contain high amounts of sugar.
- Whole Grains: Keto is a gluten-free diet, as gluten is simple carbohydrates.

- Processed foods: Other than the additives that are included, these are generally based on sugars and carbs.
- Sugars: As a general rule, all sugar is going to be cut. Do not fret. There are some great substitutions we will talk about soon.

How to Track Your Macronutrients

It is important to know that you must keep your macronutrients in balance. For instance, you must have a low amount of carbohydrate intake when you are consuming more healthy fats. If you keep your carb intake high along with the fats, you are still ingesting a standard American diet.

There is also a requirement to eat the correct amount of proteins and calories as well. Where do you start, you may wonder? Do not worry. With the main ingredients in the fat bombs you are going to be creating, they are loaded with the healthy macronutrients that will give you the benefits to your health that you desire without much effort.

You may have heard about macronutrients, which are the proteins, fats, and carbs that we consume. You will find yourself reading these on the nutritional label more than calories. However, as mentioned above, calories also play a role, so they must not be ignored.

As a rule, most people who start the Keto Diet will set their macros to be 20% protein, 5% carbs, and 75% fat intake. This is for someone who is in a relatively healthy state, which most people are not at that level when they start. It is okay. Just know that every body is different, and yours is not an exception.

If you are exercising, have medical concerns, or overweight, the macronutrients you need to consume may be drastically different. The best way to find what works for your body is to calculate your body mass and weight.

The easiest way to figure your specific macros is to go to an online calculator that will figure all the complicated formulas to derive your numbers for Basal Metabolic Rate (BMR), your current activity levels, and your Body Fat Percentage leading you to find out your Lean Muscle Mass. These are all essential in finding out what foods you need to consume to keep your body in Ketosis.

Once you find out your numbers, it will tell you what percentage of fats, carbs, and proteins you need to ingest including calories. Generally, if you are trying to lose weight, you will be consuming approximately 20% fewer calories than you consume and changing the way you eat by limiting carbs and significantly raising the number of healthy fats you consume.

As a note, it is rather dangerous to decrease your regular calorie intake by 30% or more over a long-term period. You will put yourself more at risk for health issues. As explained, there is a balance that must be followed, but once you have your numbers, it will be a breeze.

Nutritional Information Note for this cookbook

Nutritional information for the recipes provided is an approximate only. Moreover, substitutions that you use will alter the nutritional values and need to be researched personally to stay on track with the Keto diet. As such, we cannot guarantee the complete accuracy of the nutritional information given for any recipe in this cookbook. Erythritol carbs are not included in the net carb counts, as it has been shown not to impact blood sugar. The method that net carbs are calculated is the total amount of carbs minus the fiber.

Chapter 2: All about Fat Bombs

What are the Fat Bombs?

This is essentially the perfect name because it describes these snacks quite correctly. These usually small treats are packed comprising of approximately 85% healthy fats, have a varying degree of proteins, and are always low in carbs. They will surprisingly fill you up despite the size. Just know that you are not going to be living off them during your Keto diet, and you cannot pop them in your mouth like you used to with that bag of gumdrops.

They are usually very quick and easy to make which is why they are quite popular in the Keto diet and all the rage. They have savory and sweet ones, so that you can enjoy them even for breakfast, dinner, or any time in between.

You will find the main ingredients will be coconut butter and oil, sweeteners, and cream cheese, but they vary in size and shape to satisfy everyone's taste buds. If you are going to become a Fat Bomb Queen or King, you are certainly going to want to invest in some silicone molds of different varieties, but do not worry. You do not have to make the switch right away as you can still use the old-fashioned muffin tin and baking cups as well.

Health Benefits and Advantages

One of the benefits of these morsels is they will give you the energetic fat that you need especially if you don't have the time to bake a meal or you are craving a snack. The fat bomb is a perfect solution to these. They can even be eaten before or after a workout. Do not let the size fool you. They alone will keep you going for hours.

Have you just craved secretly grabbing a candy bar at the convenience store? Well, the fat bomb is, yet again, the answer. You might be surprised at the recipes that will mimic or even taste better than your usual go-to at the store. Also, they are a much healthier choice for you.

You also can take them anywhere because of their size. They can be wrapped with plastic or kept in a small container and easily thrown into a bag. Just be careful with the ones based in coconut oil if you are in a warm place, as they will melt!

Remember, you are not going to be eating any more sugars, so these sweet treats are substituting healthy natural sweeteners to satisfy your nagging sweet tooth. This also keeps your blood sugar in check.

Tips on Ingredients

Some main ingredients are an absolute necessity in the Keto diet to have the high-fat content that you need instead of the carbs. The following is an overview of the main ingredients that you will need to stock your pantry with to adjust more easily to the Keto diet.

Butter

Some of the recipes call for these butters specifically, but you can substitute any butter you wish instead of using traditional butter if you prefer.

Almond butter, in its pure form, is simply ground-roasted or raw almonds. It is a much healthier alternative to regular butter as there are no additives like sugar and it has 3 grams of net carbohydrates per serving. This is an ingredient to keep a close on the ingredients list, as they like to add less desirable contents, especially in the cheaper brands. If you want to avoid this completely, stick with the organic brands, as they will generally have no more than two ingredients in totality.

Cacao butter is an excellent butter for people with health concerns with inflammation as it decreases quite rapidly after consuming. This is called for in recipes more for the chocolate factor, but you must know that there are added benefits other than taste that is included in the fat bomb recipes.

Coconut butter is a perfect choice for people who have lactose intolerance or a dairy allergy. It also has extremely high antibacterial benefits and keeps many common illnesses at bay such as upper respiratory infections. On the other hand, it assists in treating diseases including the heavy hitters of cancer and diabetes. This is due to the amount of lauric acid and medium-chain fatty acids that coconut butter contains. Also, being an excellent source of iron and fiber, you really cannot go wrong to make the switch to this wonderful alternative to regular butter.

Coconut oil can be used as a substitute in these recipes instead of butter. This is a good choice for people who had lactose intolerance or a dairy allergy.

Most of the recipes call for melted coconut oil. The best way to do this is to use a saucepan to boil some water. Once at the boiling point, lower the burner to low heat and place the jar of coconut oil inside. Stir the mixture frequently until liquefied.

Flours
Almond flour is quite popular in the Keto diet as the main substitute for the traditional wheat flours. It has a much higher fat content than wheat flour, which tends to burn recipes much quicker.

Because almond flour is made just from almonds, you can make it right in your kitchen. All you would need is a high-powered blender to pulverize the almonds.
As a rule of thumb, when you are converting old-fashioned recipes, you should use 50% more almond flour versus the amount of traditional wheat flour.

Coconut flour has extremely high levels of saturated which aid in metabolism and assist in naturally balancing out your blood sugar levels. Coconut flour has many other benefits such as being high in fiber, low in carbs and sugar, and is incredibly packed with vitamins and minerals.

Because coconut flour is more absorbent, you will need only small amounts in these recipes, and it will keep you satisfied for much longer compared to traditional flour.

Most people prefer the compliment it has in taste for the fruity fat bomb and snack recipes.

Sweeteners

There are many types of sweeteners on the market today. Only Stevia (also known as Erythritol) and Swerve are used in this cookbook, because they are the best choices according to many scientific studies concerning the Keto diet.They contain no carbs or sugars and are calorie free!

Swerve has the benefit of aiding your health by lowering inflammation and reducing blood pressure. It has also been shown to level out the glucose and insulin present in the blood for everyone who consumes Swerve, especially for people living with diabetes.It has also shown results for patients with heart disease and obesity complications.

Erythritol also is beneficial especially for diabetes patients as it enhances the function of the blood vessels. In turn, this helps people with complications of heart disease as well. It also does not affect insulin or blood sugar levels.Erythritol also aids in preventing a buildup of plaque on the teeth.

The types of sweeteners used in these recipes include:
Stevia liquid drops can also be used as a substitute in a pinch for the confectioner sugar. For every 2 teaspoons of sweetener, you can substitute 7 drops of Stevia liquid sweetener.

Swerve is just as sweet as the sugar you are used to in grandma's recipes and even measures the same.
Stevia is a natural sweetener that derives from the stevia plant and is found in melons and grapes naturally as well. The more common name of Erythritol also knows this.

Making Tasty but Cheap Fat Bombs
Time Saving Tips

The biggest time-saving tip is you can double these recipes, as the ones that do not require being in the freezer will stay fresh on the counter for approximately 5 days if kept in a lidded tub. Most of the recipes will keep in the refrigerator for up to 1 week and up 3 months in the freezer!! If there are any variations to these guidelines, it will say it specifically in the recipe.

If you chose to store them in the fridge, simply wrap each ball securely in plastic wrap, put them in a sealed container, or throw them into a zip-lock plastic bag. If you are storing them in the freezer, be sure to put them in a freezer safe container or zip-lock bag.

If they are frozen, simply pull them out approximately 10 minutes before you want to eat them, and you can consume the fat bombs straight out of the fridge or from the counter.

Another alternative to using candy or muffin cups if you are using the muffin tin, is to brush the inside of each cup with melted coconut oil. Then harden the oil by freezing for at least 20 minutes, and this will ensure the fat bombs will not stick. This will come in handy as many of the recipes in Keto stick to the pan due to the alternative ingredients used.

Do not feel like you have to be the only one in the kitchen as these recipes are so simple your children can do it! So it would be good to consider letting the kids make the simple ones and work together with them on the more complex recipes. This will also give you more time with your family while helping them build healthy eating habits and have a better relationship with food.

Money Saving Tips:

You will find that the ingredients that are called for in the Keto diet recipes are going to be more expensive. Luckily, there are many ways to cut down on the costs, and here is a basic guideline to ensure you have the best tasting fat bombs and still have money in your pocket at the end of the day.

The best thing to do is research and shop around for the best prices. Do not blindly buy the cheapest items because they do sometimes have additives that you most likely would not want to have in your new lifestyle or are downright against the Keto diet. So, read the ingredients lists to ensure you are getting what you actually want.

You can also cut costs by making some of the main ingredients yourself. The best addition to your kitchen, if you do not already own one, is a high-powered blender or coffee grinder. To make the almond and coconut flours, you simply put in almonds and coconut meat, respectively, and grind until powdered. It is easy as that, and you will not need to bother with going to the store for these items.

If creating your own flour is too much of a hassle, you can alternatively look at purchasing flax meal, nut flours, or almond meal as a flour substitute. It is about half the cost of the almond flour in the store and is still loaded with all the macros and nutrients your body needs.

If you are finding that you are constantly buying certain items, consider buying them in bulk. It may be a little bit more money at the front, but it will save you money in the long run and save you time from having to take trips to the market.

Even thinking about buying blocked cheese and shredding yourself or buying meat that is on sale and freezing for later fat bombs and meals. Just be sure to label it so you know what date it should be consumed by.

Alternatively, you can look for online retailers such as Amazon.com and cut out the trip to the grocery store altogether. Your ingredients will be delivered straight to your door, and you can even set up an automated delivery for common items you use.

There are many benefits to purchasing organic and grass-fed meats and butters, but these are not absolutely necessary. If you compare the ingredients that you now will use in the Keto diet compared to your eating habits before, chances are you are making more healthy choices overall. Don't stress if you are not able to afford a fancy item, as there are cheaper alternatives out there if you educate yourself. The key is to look at the ingredients list of everything that you buy to ensure there are no additives that will keep you from your personal goals.

This next tip is a time and money saver. You can double any of these recipes or even save the leftovers for eating the next day or later. This will make sure that you do not have to cook for every snack, and you will have time to make other fat bombs.

As you get more accustomed to your new lifestyle, you will find you will naturally spend less money. This is because even these sweet treats will leave you satisfied for longer, so you do not have to keep buying food because you have a sugar crash or craving. As the basis of the Keto diet is to pack up the healthy fats in your daily diet, you will find that the portions you will want to eat will be less as well.

Most of these recipes require some cupcake tin or mold. Personally, you should consider investing at least one or two molds, as they will end up saving you time and money in the end. You won't need to purchase continuously baking lining and muffin cups, and the cleanup is extremely easy. You will fall in love with the silicone products once you introduce them into your kitchen if you have not already.

Chapter 3: Sweet Fat Bomb Recipes

Almond Coconut Fat Bomb

With only three ingredients, it does not get much easier than this! You are on the fast track to eating a healthy snack in no time.

Cooking Time & Total Prep Time: 5 minutes
Makes: 24 Fat Bombs
Calories: 72
Sugar: 0 grams
Fat: 8 grams
Net Carbs: 2 grams
Protein: 2 grams

What you need:

- 2 c. chocolate chips, unsweetened
- One-fourth c. coconut butter, softened

- 24 almonds, raw and whole (approximately one-fourth c.)
  - One-half c. chocolate chips, unsweetened and separate

Steps:

1. Use a non-stick muffin mold with 12 cups. Alternatively, you can use a 24-cup mini tin.
2. In a saucepan, liquefy the 2 c. of chocolate chips. Once melted, distribute to chocolate to the muffin cups.
3. Transfer the muffin pan to the fridge for half an hour or until set.
4. Remove when firm and spoon the coconut butter evenly above the hardened chocolate. Leave enough room for an additional layer of chocolate.
5. The rest of the chocolate chips (half c.) should be melted and pour the remaining layer on the coconut butter.
6. Press a whole almond onto each fat bomb and transfer to the fridge to harden for approximately 30 additional minutes.

7. Any leftovers may be kept in the fridge or freezer in a lidded container.
    Variation Tip:

- You can mix and match with the nuts you use in this recipe. Walnuts and pecans are recommended as they have a lower carb count compared to cashews.

Carrot Cake Fat Bomb

That is right! You do not have to give up the celebrations; meaning you can actually have your cake and eat it too.

Cooking Time & Total Prep Time: 1 hour 15 minutes
Makes: 45 Fat Bombs
Calories: 80
Sugar: 0 grams
Fat: 8 grams
Net Carbs: 0.9 grams
Protein: 1 gram

What you need:

- one-half c. cream cheese, softened
- 2 t. ground cinnamon
- one-half c. butter, salted and softened

- 2 T. flax meal
- 1 c. coconut butter, melted
- 6 oz. carrots, grated
- 1 c. walnuts, chopped

Steps:

1. Set aside a prepared flat sheet with baking lining or utilize a silicone mat.
2. Using a food blender, pulse the flax meal, cream cheese, and butter until combined.
3. Blend in the butter, grated carrots, and coconut butter until incorporated.
4. Spoon out with a 1-inch cookie scoop and roll into 45 individual balls and transfer to the prepared pan.
5. Dust the balls with cinnamon and walnuts, evenly coating the top. Press lightly into the balls to cling the coating to each.
6. Serve and enjoy!
    Baking Tip:

- If the dough is too soft to roll, place in the fridge until thickened.

Chai Fat Bomb

Enjoy these with your morning or afternoon coffee and be transported to Asia in only 5 minutes.

Cooking Time & Total Prep Time: 5 minutes
Makes: 14 Fat Bombs
Calories: 45
Protein: 1 gram
Sugar: 0 grams
Fat: 5 grams
Net Carbs: 0.2 grams

What you need:

- 2 tea bags chai or spiced blend
- 1 oz. butter, softened
- 2 T. coconut oil

- 1 oz. coconut butter, softened

Steps:

1. Place a 14-cup non-stick candy mold to the side.
2. Dissolve the coconut butter, butter, and coconut oil in a saucepan, mixing occasionally until incorporated.
3. Distribute the mixture to the candy mold and freeze for one hour.
4. Remove approximately 10 minutes before serving and enjoy!

Chocolate Brownie Fat Bomb

You will not be able to taste the difference with this raw brownie recipe, as it will still melt in your mouth.
Cooking Time & Total Prep Time: 10 minutes
Makes: 24 Fat Bombs
Calories: 110
Sugar: 1 gram
Fat: 10 grams
Net Carbs: 2 grams
Protein: 2 grams

What you need:

- 1 c. coconut butter, softened
- 2 T. cacao, powdered and unsweetened
- one-half c. almond flour
- 2 oz. pistachios, peeled and chopped
- 1 t. vanilla extract, sugar-free

- 3 tbs. coconut oil, melted

Steps:

1. Place a regular-sized glass baking dish to the side.
2. In a glass dish, blend the coconut butter, cacao powder, vanilla extract, and coconut oil until integrated.
3. Evenly press the mixture into the base of the glass dish. The pistachios should be sprinkled on top and lightly depressed into the batter.
4. Move the baking dish to the refrigerator for approximately half an hour. Remove and cut into 1-inch squares.
5. Serve and enjoy!

Chocolate Cherry Fat Bomb

These fat bombs are loaded with healthy coconut oil and will satisfy your sweet tooth as the cherries explode in your mouth.
Cooking Time & Total Prep Time: 1 hour 10 minutes
Makes: 12 Fat Bombs
Protein: 0 grams
Net Carbs: 1 gram
Fat: 6 grams
Sugar: 1 gram
Calories: 67

What you need:

- one-half t. vanilla extract, sugar-free
- three-fourth c. sweet cherries
- one-half t. almond extract, sugar-free
    - 5 drops Stevia liquid
- one-fourth c. coconut butter, melted

- 3 T. cacao, unsweetened and powdered
- one-fourth c. coconut oil, melted

Steps:

1. You will need an ice cube tray or a mini muffin tin with baking cups prepared and set to the side.
2. Using a food blender, blend the coconut oil, powdered cacao, and coconut butter until completely melded together.
3. Mix in the vanilla extract, almond extract, and liquid Stevia until blended.
4. In a glass dish, crush the cherries with a masher or fork. Fold the cherry juice and mashed cherries into the batter.
5. Spoon out into the prepared trays and freeze for approximately one hour until set.
6. Serve and enjoy!

Chocolate Coconut Oil Fat Bomb

Get your daily dose of coconut oil with a chocolaty sensation that is sure to be on top of your favorites list.

Cooking Time & Total Prep Time: 1 hour 10 minutes
Makes: 12 Fat Bombs
Protein: 1 gram
Net Carbs: 1 gram
Fat: 16 grams
Sugar: 0 grams
Calories: 122

What you need:

- one-half c. cacao, unsweetened and powdered
- three-fourth c. coconut oil, melted
- 8 drops Stevia liquid
- one-half T. salt
- 3 T. cacao nibs, unsweetened
- Coconut oil spray

Steps:

1. Coat a regular-sized muffin tin with coconut oil spray and set to the side.
2. Using a food blender, whisk the Stevia, powdered cacao, and coconut oil until integrated.
3. Evenly transfer the batter to the muffin cups. Use salt and cacao nibs to dust. The covering should be lightly pressed into the batter.
4. Move the tray to the freezer for approximately 60 minutes and store in the freezer in a zip-lock bag until ready to serve.

   Variation Tip:

- To add some flavor, add one teaspoon of turmeric or cinnamon into the batter.

Chocolate Fat Bomb

This is one of the classics, but whoever has forgotten their first bite into a piece of decadent chocolate?

Cooking Time & Total Prep Time: 45 minutes
Makes: 6 Fat Bombs
Protein: 8 grams
Net Carbs: 4.1 grams
Fat: 34 grams
Sugar: 0 grams
Calories: 388

What you need:

- one-fourth c. cocoa, unsweetened and powdered
- 5 T. peanut butter, chunky
- one-half c. coconut oil

- 2 T. Stevia sweetener, granulated
- 6 T. hemp seeds, shelled
- 1 t. vanilla extract, sugar-free
- 2 T. heavy cream

Steps:

1. Layer a regular-sized flat pan with baking lining or use a non-stick mat.
2. In a big dish, whip the peanut butter, hemp seeds, and cocoa powder until combined.
3. Blend in the coconut oil and heavy cream until the consistency is a thick paste.
4. Stir in the Stevia and vanilla extract until incorporated.
5. Use a cookie scoop in spooning the batter. Create individual balls, around 12 pieces, and then put them on the prepared pan.
6. Refrigerate for half an hour to set and serve.

Creamed Blueberry Fat Bomb

This is a great spring or summer treat that will make you think you have a bowl of blueberries and cream in your mouth.

Cooking Time & Total Prep Time: 10 minutes
Makes: 30 Fat Bombs
Protein: 1 gram
Net Carbs: 1 gram
Fat: 4 grams
Sugar: 0 grams
Calories: 48

What you need:

- one-fourth c. coconut, unsweetened and shredded
- one-half t. Stevia sweetener, granulated
- one-half c. pecans, raw
- 1 t. vanilla extract, sugar-free

- 1 c. almond flour
- one-half c. blueberries
- 4 oz. goat cheese, softened

Steps:

1. In a food blender, whip the goat cheese, almond flour, and Stevia until well combined.
2. Slowly incorporate the blueberries, pecans, and vanilla extract until the batter is thick.
3. In a small dish or plate, add the shredded coconut.
4. Create 30 individual balls and fully cover them with the coconut by rolling in them.
5. Place on a serving plate and enjoy!

Danish Butter Cookie Fat Bomb

These fat bombs are full of healthy fats, which will boost your energy levels as the tastes of sweet and buttery meld together in your mouth.

Cooking Time & Total Prep Time: 10 minutes
Makes: 8 Fat Bombs
Protein: 4 grams
Net Carbs: 1.6 grams
Fat: 10grams
Sugar: 0 grams
Calories: 114

What you need:

- 1 t. vanilla extract, sugar-free
- 3 T. butter, melted
- 1 c. almond flour
- 2 T. Swerve sweetener, granulated

- one-eight t. salt

Steps:

1. Prepare a flat sheet layered with baking lining or use a non-stick silicone mat. Set to the side.
2. Using a regular dish, whisk the Swerve, melted butter, vanilla extract, almond flour, and salt until thickened.
3. Roll into eight equally-sized balls and place on the prepped pan.
4. Firm the fat bombs in the fridge for 60 minutes or serve immediately.

Ginger Fat Bomb

These Ginger Fat bombs are loaded with coconut oil and fats, which keep you fuller for longer.

Cooking Time & Total Prep Time: 40 minutes
Makes: 10 Fat Bombs
Calories: 120
Sugar: 0.1 grams
Fat: 13 grams
Net Carbs: 0.8 grams
Protein: 1 gram

What you need:

- one-fourth c. coconut, unsweetened and shredded
- 3 oz. coconut butter, softened
- 1 t. Swerve sweetener, granulated
- 3 oz. coconut oil, softened

- 1 t. ginger, powdered

Steps:

1. Set an ice cube tray or silicone mold to the side.
2. In a blender, pulse the shredded coconut, Swerve, and coconut butter for approximately half a minute on high.
3. Combine the coconut oil and ginger for an additional half minute until incorporated fully.
4. Transfer the mixture to the prepped mold. For thirty minutes, chill in the fridge before serving.

Hazelnut Fat Bomb

These fat bombs couple wonderfully with your daily coffee or just as an afternoon snack to keep you going under dinnertime.

Cooking Time & Total Prep Time: 25 minutes
Makes: 10 Fat Bombs
Fat: 14 grams
Net Carbs: 1.2 gram
Protein: 2 grams
Sugar: 0 grams
Calories: 140

What you need:

- Three-fourth c. hazelnuts, ground
- 2 T. Erythritol, confectioner

- 3 T. coconut oil, melted
- 1 oz. chocolate, unsweetened and melted
- 8 oz. hazelnuts, chopped
- one-half T. cacao powder, unsweetened and ditched
- 10 hazelnuts, raw and whole
- one-half t. vanilla extract, sugar-free

Steps:

1. In a saucepan, dissolve the chocolate and coconut oil together, mixing often. Remove from heat.
2. Using a food blender, pulse the ground hazelnuts, Erythritol, and powdered cacao for approximately 45 seconds on high.
3. Scrape the dish before combining the melted chocolate and vanilla extract and pulse for an additional half minute.
4. Freeze for approximately 15 minutes and remove.
5. Pour the chopped hazelnuts on a plate or dish.
6. As you are rolling each ball, place a whole hazelnut inside. Fully cover with the chopped hazelnuts
7. Serve immediately and enjoy!

Baking Tip:

- The chocolate you ideally need to use in this recipe will need to contain at least 85% cacao.

Mocha Peppermint Fat Bomb

A perfect morning starts with this fat bomb, loaded with caffeine and minty goodness full of the fats you need to get going.

Cooking Time & Total Prep Time: 10 minutes
Makes: 6 Fat Bombs
Fat: 18 grams
Net Carbs: 1 gram
Protein: 2 grams
Sugar: 0 grams
Calories: 84

What you need:

For the fat bomb:

- one-half t. cocoa, unsweetened and powdered
- 2 T. coconut oil, melted
- one-half t. instant coffee
- 2 T. Swerve sweetener, granulated
- 1 t. hot water

- 3 T. almond flour
- One-eighth t. mint extract, sugar-free

For the coating:

- 1 t. cocoa, unsweetened and powdered
- One and one-half t. Swerve sweetener, granulated

Steps:

1. In a small dish, blend the coffee and hot water and stir until the coffee granules are completely dissolved.
2. Using a food blender, pulse the Swerve, cacao powder, coconut oil, and mint extract until thoroughly combined.
3. Integrate the coffee and almond flour until the batter thickens.
4. Freeze for approximately 10 minutes.
5. In a glass dish, blend the Swerve and cocoa powder until incorporated.
6. Remove the dish from the freezer, and roll into six individual balls.
7. Cover each ball completely with the coating and serve immediately.

8. For any leftovers, transfer to the refrigerator in a sealed tub and they will keep fresh for 5 days.

Baking Tip:

- If you do not need the extra kick, you can substitute the instant coffee for decaffeinated coffee.

Orange Fat Bomb

These Orange Fat bombs are creamy, and the citrus will bite at your tongue.
Cooking Time & Total Prep Time: 10 minutes
Makes: 6 Fat Bombs
Protein: 0 grams
Net Carbs: 2 grams
Fat: 7 grams
Sugar: 0 grams
Calories: 71

What you need:

- one-fourth c. Swerve sweetener, confectioner
- 2 T. butter
- 2 oz. heavy cream
- One-fourth c. coconut oil, melted and cooled
- 4 oz. cream cheese

- one-half T. orange zest

Steps:

1. Layer a flat sheet with baking lining or use a glass baking dish. Set aside.
2. Using a food blender, whip the Swerve and cream cheese together for approximately 2 minutes.
3. Combine the butter and coconut oil and pulse for half a minute.
4. Finally, blend the heavy cream and orange zest and beat for 60 seconds.
5. Roll into 6 individual balls and distribute to the prepped pan.
6. Freeze for approximately 60 minutes and remove 10 minutes before serving.

Baking Tip:

- Alternatively, you can use a non-stick silicone mold instead of rolling into individual balls.

Peanut Butter Fat Bomb

This fat bomb recipe will remind you of the peanut butter cups that you used to eat. In fact, you will not taste the difference.

Cooking Time & Total Prep Time: 2 hours 10 minutes
Makes: 12 Fat Bombs
Protein: 1 gram
Net Carbs: 1 gram
Fat: 16 grams
Sugar: 0 grams
Calories: 161

What you need:

- 2 T. Swerve sweetener, granulated
- 1 t. vanilla extract, sugar-free
- 2 c. heavy whipping cream
- 3 T. peanut butter

Steps:

1. Place a silicone cupcake mold or use a standard muffin tray with baking cups. Set to the side.
2. In a glass dish, whisk the heavy whipping cream and vanilla extract for 4 minutes using an electrical beater.
3. Integrate the Swerve and peanut butter and completely combine for an additional 3 minutes.
4. Spoon the whipped mixture into a piping bag and squeeze the contents equally into the cups.
5. Freeze for 2 hours and enjoy!

Variation Tip:

- Alternatively, you can press one-half cup of unsweetened dark chocolate chips or crushed peanuts onto the top before you transfer to the freezer.

Peppermint Andes Fat Bomb

It is hard to believe these Peppermint Andes Fat Bombs have no sugar because they taste like the real thing.
Cooking Time & Total Prep Time: 1 hour 30 minutes
Makes: 6 Fat Bombs
Protein: 1 gram
Net Carbs: 0.5 gram
Fat: 21 grams
Sugar: 0 grams
Calories: 200

What you need:

- 1 c. coconut oil, melted and cooled
- 1 T. Swerve sweetener, confectioner
- one-fourth t. peppermint extract, sugar-free
- 2 T. cocoa, unsweetened

Steps:

1. You will need to set aside a silicon non-stick candy mold or ice cube tray.
2. In a glass dish, blend the one-half c. of the melted coconut oil and peppermint extract until combined.
3. Evenly distribute to the mold and transfer to the fridge for half an hour.
4. Using an additional glass dish, combine the cocoa powder, Swerve, and the remaining one-half c. of melted coconut oil until well blended.
5. Remove the mold from the refrigerator and empty the chocolate mixture into each section.
6. Refrigerate for an additional 45 minutes before serving.

Red Velvet Fat Bomb

One of the favorite classics that cannot be beaten; this fat bomb keeps your macros in check by having no carbs!

Cooking Time & Total Prep Time: 1 hour
Makes: 24 Fat Bombs
Protein: 0 grams
Net Carbs: 0 grams
Fat: 6 grams
Sugar: 0 grams
Calories: 59

What you need:

For the fat bomb:

- 3 T. Swerve sweetener, granulated
- 1 t. vanilla extract, sugar-free
- 3.5-oz. butter, softened
- one-half c. cream cheese, softened

- 3.5-oz. dark chocolate, unsweetened

For the whipped cream:

- 2 t. Erythritol
- one-third c. heavy cream
- 4 drops red food coloring

Steps:

1. Arrange 2 cupcake tins by lining with baking cups or use a silicone candy mold. Set to the side.
2. Using a saucepan, liquefy the chocolate, often stirring to ensure it does not burn.
3. Meanwhile, in a glass dish, blend the butter, Swerve, cream cheese, and vanilla extract with an electrical beater until combined.
4. Slowly beat the melted chocolate to the mixture until incorporated fully.
5. Spoon into a piping bag and evenly transfer the contents into the prepped mold.
6. Move to the fridge for 45 minutes to set the fat bombs.
7. In a separate glass dish, whip the Erythritol, food coloring, and heavy cream for 5 minutes with an

electrical beater. Scoop the whipped cream into a piping bag.

8. Remove the fat bombs from the refrigerator, top with whipped cream, and serve
   Baking Tip:

- If you do not own a piping bag, you can alternatively use a large zip-lock bag. Simply cut the end of one corner of the bottom and you have a do it yourself pastry bag!

Chapter 4: Savory Fat Bomb Recipes
Alfredo Fat Bomb

Take a trip to Italy by munching on some fat bombs that will leave you satisfied, but you will be looking forward to having more.

Cooking Time & Total Prep Time: 2 hours 10 minutes
Makes: 6 Fat Bombs
Calories: 97
Protein: 2 grams
Sugar: 0.8 grams
Fat: 9 grams
Net Carbs: 1.5 grams

What you need:

- One-eighth t. pepper
- 8 oz. cream cheese

- one-fourth t. salt
- 2 T. parsley, fresh and chopped finely
- One-eighth t. Italian seasoning
- 3 t. butter, softened
- 1 t. garlic powder
- 3 T. parmesan cheese, grated

Steps:

1. Use a non-stick mat or layer baking liner on a flat sheet. Set to the side.
2. In a glass dish, use an electrical beater to combine the butter and cream cheese.
3. Blend the garlic powder and grated parmesan cheese until completely combined.
4. Fold the salt, Italian seasoning, and parsley until integrated and refrigerate for approximately 60 minutes.
5. Remove the batter and equally divide and roll into six individual balls.
6. Refrigerate for an additional hour before serving.

Avocado & Ham Fat Bomb

This quick recipe will certainly keep your taste buds happy along with your energy levels.

Cooking Time & Total Prep Time: 5 minutes
Makes: 10 Fat Bombs
Protein: 8 grams
Net Carbs: 0 grams
Fat: 6 grams
Sugar: 0 grams
Calories: 90

What you need:

- 1 avocado
- 10 slices deli ham
- 1 lime

Steps:

1. On a serving plate, lay out the slices of ham to lay flat.

2. Slice the avocado in two and divide into 10 sections. Cut open the lime and squeeze the juice over the cuts of avocado.
3. Transfer the avocado to the ham slices, roll into a tube, and enjoy!
    Variation Tip:

- Alternatively, you can use prosciutto or deli turkey for this recipe.

Barbeque Chicken Fat Bomb

You do not have to give up the good stuff on the Keto diet, and this savory fat bomb will not disappoint.

Cooking Time & Total Prep Time: 1 hour
Makes: 10 Fat Bombs
Calories: 164
Sugar: 1 gram
Fat: 12 grams
Net Carbs: 0.8 grams
Protein: 8 grams

What you need:

- 5 chicken breasts, skinless and boneless
- One-eighth t. salt
- 5 medium jalapenos, sliced in halves and seedless
- One-fourth t. pepper
- 4 oz. cream cheese, softened 1 c. cheddar cheese, shredded

- 20 slices bacon, uncooked
- 1 c. barbecue sauce, sugar-free

Steps:

1. Slice the chicken breast into halves. Sandwich between two pieces of baking paper and beat with a mallet until approximately one-fourth-inch thick.
2. Use pepper and salt and sprinkle the meat.
3. Set the stove to preheat to the temperature of 400° Fahrenheit. Cover two rimmed flat sheets with aluminum foil and place to the side.
4. In a glass dish, blend the shredded cheddar cheese and cream cheese until combined.
5. Spread the jalapeno halves with the cheese mixture then place each on top of the flattened chicken. Rotate the chicken around the jalapeno creating a roll.
6. Each piece of chicken should be wrapped around with a slice of bacon. Repeat with another piece of bacon wrapping the opposite direction. Move the wrapped fat bombs to one of the prepped pans.

7. Heat for 10 minutes and then flip the fat bombs over and keep in the stove for another 10 minutes.
8. Remove the baked chicken and transfer to the other prepped pan. Reduce the stove temperature to 375° Fahrenheit.
9. Using a pastry brush, spread the barbecue sauce over the entire fat bomb by turning over, ensuring it is fully covered.
10. Heat for an additional 6 minutes and remove. Apply additional barbeque sauce over the top.
11. Set the stove to the broil setting for three minutes and remove from heat.
12. Wait for 10 minutes before serving.
    Variation tip:

- You can also use 10 fillets for this recipe in place of the boneless chicken breasts.

Buttery Bacon Fat Bomb

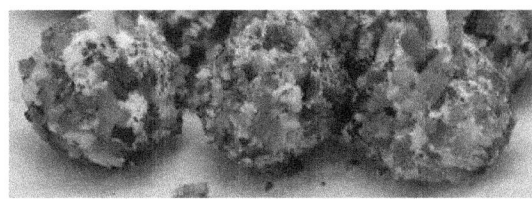

These are a wonderful breakfast treat, as you cannot go wrong with bacon in the morning or the afternoon for that matter.
Cooking Time & Total Prep Time: 50 minutes
Makes: 6 Fat Bombs
Protein: 5 grams
Net Carbs: 1 gram
Fat: 18 grams
Sugar: 0 grams
Calories: 183

What you need:

- 1 large egg, hardboiled
- 3 oz. avocado
- 1 medium jalapeno pepper, seeded and diced
- 4 T. butter, unsalted
- 1 T. mayonnaise
- 2 T. bacon grease

- One-eighth t. salt
- One-fourth t. pepper
- Three-fourth t. lime juice
- 6 bacon slices
- 1 T. cilantro, chopped
- 2 T. coconut oil

Steps:

1. In a skillet, brown the bacon until crispy using the coconut oil. Use paper towels to cover a plate so the excess grease can be soaked up after removing from the heat.
2. In a big glass dish, blend the mayonnaise, butter, and avocado until combined.
3. Integrate the hardboiled egg, jalapeno pepper, bacon grease, and cilantro, blending until incorporated fully.
4. Flavor the mixture with salt, lime juice, and pepper and refrigerate for half an hour.
5. In a dish, crush the bacon into small chunks and remove the batter.

6. Divide into 6 equal sections and form a ball. Roll the balls in the bacon bits fully. Serve and enjoy!

Cauliflower Cheese Fat Bomb

Another fat packed recipe that has been transformed into a brilliant mix of vegetables and cheese.
Cooking Time & Total Prep Time: 5 hours
Makes: 30 Fat Bombs
Protein: 6 grams
Net Carbs: 1.8 grams
Fat: 6 grams
Sugar: 0 grams
Calories: 93

What you need:

- 1 t. garlic powder
- 5 c. cauliflower
- one-half t. salt

- 12 oz. parmesan cheese, grated and divided
- 1 t. Italian seasoning, divided
- 16 oz. bacon
- 4 oz. goat cheese
- one-half t. pepper
- 8 oz. cheddar cheese, sharp
- 1 t. onion powder
- 3 cloves garlic, minced
- 12 oz. pork rinds, crushed
- 2 T. coconut oil, separate
- 1 c. coconut oil
- 8 oz. cream cheese, softened

Steps:

1. In a skillet, heat 2 tablespoons of coconut oil and brown the bacon until crispy. After removing from the heat, cool for ten minutes in a plate covered with paper towels.
2. Use a cheese grater to rice the cauliflower and transfer to a glass dish.

3. Combine the cream cheese, goat cheese, one-half teaspoon of Italian seasoning, and pepper until fully integrated.
4. Incorporate the cheddar cheese, salt, and parmesan cheese until blended.
5. Finally, crumble the cooked bacon into the batter and mix completely.
6. Refrigerate for 60 minutes to firm the mixture.
7. Prepare a flat sheet with a layer of baking lining and set aside.
8. Remove the batter from the fridge and roll 30 individual balls approximately 2-inches thick. Place on the prepped flat sheet and freeze for 3 hours.
9. Once ready to cook, remove the fat bombs from the freezer and set to the side.
10. In a glass dish, blend the pork rinds, one-half teaspoon of Italian seasoning, and 1 c. of parmesan cheese in a glass dish.
11. Spice with onion powder and garlic powder and blend thoroughly.

12. Heat a non-stick skillet with the remaining cup of coconut oil on medium heat.
13. Completely cover the fat bombs with the breading and transfer to the hot coconut oil for approximately 60 seconds on each side until golden.
14. Serve hot after removing from the heat and placing on a plate covered with paper towels.

Cheeseburger Fat Bomb

These are a great afternoon or even dinner fat bomb that boasts of oozing cheese.

Cooking Time & Total Prep Time: 30 minutes
Makes: 12 Fat Bombs
Protein: 8 grams
Net Carbs: 0 grams
Fat: 10 grams
Sugar: 0 grams
Calories: 125

What you need:

- 16 oz. ground beef
- one-eighth t. pepper
- 3 T. butter
- one-fourth t. salt
- 2 oz. cheese, your favorite

Steps:

1. Set the stove to preheat to the temperature of 375° Fahrenheit. Place a 12-cup silicone cupcake pan on the counter along with a flat sheet underneath.
2. In a glass dish, blend the salt, beef, and pepper until together.
3. Distribute and depress approximately 1 tablespoon of meat at the base of each cup. Spoon about one-half tablespoons of butter on each.
4. Repeat an additional 1-tablespoon layer of beef to the cups and sprinkle cheese on top.
5. Finally, top the rest of the cups with the remaining beef and compress.
6. Heat in the stove for approximately 10 minutes and turn the stove off. Open the oven door for about 5 minutes to allow to cool before removing the fat bombs.
7. Transfer each fat bomb to a serving plate with a large spoon or fork and enjoy!
    Baking Tips:

- Use the remaining butter and fat from the pans to drizzle on the cheeseburger fat bombs or to add flavoring to cooking your next vegetable meal.

Cream Cheese Fat Bomb

You might just get addicted to the simple classic that has a powerful ability to keep your cravings satisfied.
Cooking Time & Total Prep Time: 30 minutes
Makes: 6 Fat Bombs
Fat: 7 grams
Net Carbs: 1 gram
Protein: 2 grams
Sugar: 0 grams
Calories: 75

What you need:

- 1 t. Garlic, minced
- 5 oz. Cream cheese, softened

- 6 olives, chopped
- One-fourth t. Salt
- 2 T. parmesan cheese, grated

Steps:

1. In a glass dish, blend the garlic, chopped olives, cream cheese, and salt until merged.
2. Divide evenly into 6 individual balls and put into a glass baking dish. Refrigerate for approximately 15 minutes and remove.
3. Sprinkle the parmesan cheese into a bowl or plate and completely cover the fat bombs and serve.
4. The leftovers can easily be stored in the fridge for one week.

Pistachio Fat Bomb

One of the heavy hitter fat bombs that will leave you satisfied for hours.

Cooking Time & Total Prep Time: 40 minutes
Makes: 6 Fat Bombs
Protein: 1 gram
Net Carbs: 0.5 gram
Fat: 12 grams
Sugar: 0 grams
Calories: 121

What you need:

- one-half t. garlic, minced
- 8 oz. cream cheese, softened
- 2 oz. pistachios, chopped
  - 1 T. chives, minced

Steps:

1. In a glass dish, blend the cream cheese, garlic, and chives until integrated.
2. Pour the chopped pistachios into a bowl or onto a plate.
3. Roll the batter in 10 individual balls and rotate the fat bombs in the
4. Transfer to a glass baking dish and freeze for approximately half an hour and serve.
    Variation Tip:

- You do not have to use pistachios only in this recipe. Alternatively, you can use chopped cashews, pecans, walnuts, or almonds.

Pizza Fat Bomb

You can even have a "slice" of pizza as a quick snack. Make these ahead of time and just pop them out of the fridge when you are ready.

Cooking Time & Total Prep Time: 1 hour 10 minutes
Makes: 6 Fat Bombs
Net Carbs: 1.7 grams
Protein: 2 grams
Fat: 10 grams
Sugar: 0 grams
Calories: 101

What you need:

- one-half c. cream cheese
- 2 T. basil, chopped

- one-third c. pepperoni, sliced
- one-half c. olives, black and pitted
- One-eight t. pepper
- 2 T. tomato pesto
- one-fourth t. salt

Steps:

1. Chop the olives and pepperoni into small cubes.
2. In a dish, blend the tomato pesto and cream cheese until combined.
3. Add the basil and cubed pepperoni and olives until incorporated.
4. Use a cookie scooper to spoon out on a serving plate.
5. Garnish, if you prefer, with additional slices of pepperoni, olives, and basil and serve.

Sausage & Cheese Fat Bomb

These can easily be wrapped in plastic and put into your bag for your afternoon snack or even a great breakfast to start the day.
Cooking Time & Total Prep Time: 1 hour 10 minutes
Makes: 35 Fat Bombs
Fat: 10 grams
Net Carbs: 1.7 grams
Protein: 2 grams
Sugar: 0 grams
Calories: 101

What you need:

- one-fourth t. salt
- 2 T. cream cheese
- one-third c. butter, melted
- one-third c. coconut flour

- 16 oz. sausage, ground
- one-fourth t. baking powder, gluten-free
- 4 large eggs
- 2 c. cheddar cheese, shredded

Steps:

1. Set the stove to preheat to the temperature of 375° Fahrenheit. Cover a flat sheet with baking paper or aluminum foil.
2. In a saucepan, dissolve the butter completely. Remove from heat to cool.
3. Using a skillet, cook the ground sausage fully. Transfer to a paper towel covered platter to soak up grease and keep to the side.
4. In a dish, blend the cream cheese, eggs, salt, and coconut flour until combined.
5. Slowly integrate the melted butter, baking powder, and garlic until well mixed.
6. Finally, blend the cheese and cooked sausage until together.
7. Roll 35 individual balls and place on the prepped pan less than an inch apart.

8. Heat in the stove for 15 minutes and serve.
9. The leftovers can be stored for one week in the refrigerator.

Spicy Bacon & Cheese Fat Bomb

Having these for breakfast, lunch or dinner will leave you satisfied as it is absolutely packed with healthy fats to keep you going throughout the day.

Cooking Time & Total Prep Time: 2 hours 25 minutes
Makes: 6 Fat Bombs
Protein: 3 grams
Net Carbs: 1 gram
Fat: 13 grams
Sugar: 1 gram
Calories: 101

What you need:

- 8 oz. cream cheese, softened
- 4 slices bacon
- one-third c. bacon grease
- 4 oz. cheddar cheese, shredded

- 4 medium jalapeno peppers, deseeded and diced finely
- 5 oz. coconut oil, melted and divided

Steps:

1. Cover a standard-sized loaf pan with baking lining and set to the side.
2. In a skillet, brown the bacon until crispy using 2 ounces of coconut oil. Remove from burner and place on a paper towel-covered plate to soak up the excess fat.
3. In a glass dish, blend the shredded cheddar cheese, jalapeno, and cream cheese until integrated.
4. Combine the bacon grease and the remaining 3 ounces of coconut oil until blended thoroughly.
5. Empty the mixture into the prepped pan and refrigerate for 2 hours.
6. After the cheese is set, remove from the fridge and slice into 18 pieces.
7. Crush the cooked bacon into small chunks onto a small plate.

8. Roll each slice into a ball and cover the fat bombs completely in the bacon bits and serve.
9. The leftovers will keep in the freezer for one month or in the refrigerator for up to 5 days.
Baking Tip:

- If you happen to not have enough bacon grease in the pan for the recipe, combine with additional coconut oil until it equals one-third cup.

Chapter 5: Frozen Fat Bomb Recipes
Butter Cream Fat Bomb

You will not believe how easily these will melt in your mouth and will keep your tummy from rumbling for hours.

Cooking Time & Total Prep Time: 2 hours 15 minutes
Makes: 12 Fat Bombs
Protein: 1 gram
Net Carbs: 0.4 grams
Fat: 11 grams
Sugar: 0.3 grams
Calories: 102

What you need:

- one-half c. butter, softened
- 4 oz. cream cheese, softened
- 3 T. Erythritol, confectioner
- 1 t. vanilla extract, sugar-free
- 8 oz. almonds, raw and chopped
- one-eight t. salt

Steps:

1. Using a food blender, pulse the cream cheese and butter for 2 minutes.
2. Blend the sweetener, salt, and vanilla extract and continue to pulse for 8 additional minutes.
3. Spoon into a piping bag and distribute to a silicone non-stick mold and dust the top with the chopped almonds.
4. Freeze for 2 hours and remove approximately 10 minutes before serving.

   Baking Tip:

- If you do not own a piping bag, you can alternatively use a large zip-lock bag. Simply cut the end of one corner of the bottom and you have a do-it-yourself pastry bag!

Variation Tips:

- You can toast the almonds instead of keeping them raw, but you may lose some of the nutrients opting for this. To toast, place sliced almonds on a flat sheet and heat in a stove preheated to 350° Fahrenheit for approximately 3 minutes. Then you can leave them sliced or put them in a blender and pulse for about half a minute to coarsely chop.
- If you want to alternatively use dark chocolate covering or combine with the almonds, drizzle 8 ounces of melted dark chocolate over the tops before freezing.

Butter Pecan Fat Bomb

These frozen fat bombs are loaded with healthy fats and coconut oil.

Cooking Time & Total Prep Time: 20 minutes
Makes: 6 Fat Bombs
Protein: 1 gram
Net Carbs: 0.5 grams
Fat: 30 grams
Sugar: 0 grams
Calories: 287

What you need:

- 3 T. coconut oil
- one-fourth t. Swerve sweetener, granulated
- 3 T. butter, softened
- One-eight t. salt

- 3 oz. cocoa butter
- 2 T. Erythritol, confectioner
- 1 T. Erythritol, confectioner separated
- 6 oz. pecans, chopped
- one-fourth t. vanilla extract, sugar-free

Steps:

1. Prepare a non-stick muffin tin or a candy mold with 6 cups.
2. Using a saucepan, dissolve the butter, coconut oil, and cocoa butter until blended, stirring often. Remove from heat to cool.
3. Completely integrate the vanilla extract, 2 tablespoons of Erythritol, and salt into the melted mixture.
4. Place a few pecans into each muffin cup and evenly transfer the chocolate mixture into the cups. Move the mold to the freezer and remove after half an hour.
5. Any leftovers need to be kept in the freezer and removed approximately 10 minutes before serving again.

   Variation Tip:

- Alternatively, you can use hazelnuts or walnuts in this recipe.

Caramel Peanut Butter Fat Bomb

These will make you think you are popping candy bar minis instead of a high amount of healthy fats.

Cooking Time & Total Prep Time: 2 hours 10 minutes
Makes: 8 Fat Bombs
Protein: 4 grams
Net Carbs: 0.8 gram
Fat: 20 grams
Sugar: 0 grams
Calories: 208

What you need:

- 2 oz. coconut oil, melted
- one-eighth t. vanilla extract, sugar-free
- 2 T. butter, salted and melted
- 1 T. peanut butter

- 4 drops Stevia liquid
- one-eighth t. caramel extract, sugar-free
- 8 oz. peanuts, raw

Steps:

1. Have a candy or cupcake cup silicone mold ready to the side.
2. Using a food blender, whip the peanut butter, Stevia, and vanilla extract until combined.
3. Integrate the coconut oil, melted butter, and caramel extract until the consistency is creamy.
4. Evenly distribute the batter to the candy mold and dust the tops with the peanuts, pressing lightly into batter.
5. Freeze for 2 hours and remove 10 minutes before serving.

Cheesecake Fat Bomb

This classic will not leave you displeased and you can experiment rather easily with the recipe to create your favorite cheesecake flavors.

Cooking Time & Total Prep Time: 2 hours 10 minutes
Makes: 6 Fat Bombs
Protein: 3 grams
Net Carbs: 1 gram
Fat: 32 grams
Sugar: 0 grams
Calories: 208

What you need:

- 4 oz. cream cheese, softened
- one-fourth c. peanut butter, creamy
- 2 T. Swerve sweetener, granulated

Steps:

1. Cover a regular-sized flat sheet with baking lining. Alternatively, use a non-stick mat.
2. In a dish, blend the peanut butter, cream cheese, and Swerve until combined thoroughly.
3. Roll the dough into six small balls and move to the cookie pan.
4. Freeze for approximately 2 hours and remove 10 minutes before serving.
   Variation Tip:

- You can add in alternative ingredients to flavor your cheesecake fat bombs such as a one-half cup of unsweetened chocolate chips or nuts of your choice. You can also blend in 1 teaspoon of any sugar-free flavored extract such as lemon or vanilla.

Chocolate Chip Cookie Dough Fat Bomb

You cannot go wrong to have these on a sunny afternoon in the summer.

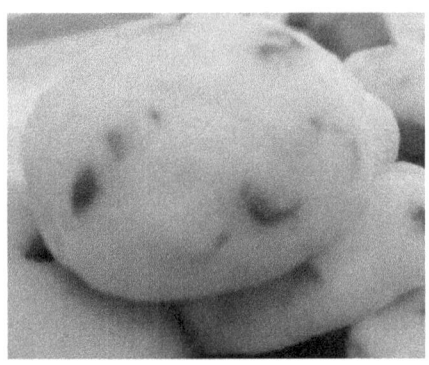

Cooking Time & Total Prep Time: 2 hours 15 minutes
Makes: 15 Fat Bombs
Protein: 2 grams
Net Carbs: 1 gram
Fat: 9 grams
Sugar: 0 grams
Calories: 90

What you need:

- one-fourth c. butter, salted and softened
- 4 oz. cream cheese, softened
- 3 oz. chocolate chips, unsweetened

- one-fourth c. peanut butter, creamy
- 3 T. Swerve sweetener, granulated
- 1 t. vanilla extract, sugar-free

Steps:

1. Layer a flat sheet with baking lining or you can use a round silicone mold. Set to the side.
2. Using a food blender, whip the butter, chocolate chips, and Swerve for 60 seconds.
3. Blend in the cream cheese, peanut butter, and vanilla extract until combined.
4. Refrigerate for approximately half an hour and remove.
5. Spoon out 15 individual balls and place on the prepped tray or transferring to the mold.
6. Freeze for about 2 hours and serve.
7. Any leftovers can be stored in a zip-lock bag in the freezer.

Chocolate Sea Salt Fat Bomb

The perfect combination of sea salt and chocolate will leave your sweet tooth beyond happy.

Cooking Time & Total Prep Time: 6 hours 20 minutes
Makes: 10 Fat Bombs
Protein: 5 grams
Net Carbs: 0.2 gram
Fat: 13 grams
Sugar: 0 grams
Calories: 141

What you need:

- 4 oz. heavy whipping cream
- 1 t. vanilla extract, sugar-free
- 4 oz. coconut oil, melted
- one-half c. sun butter

- 2 T. cocoa, powdered
- one-third c. cream cheese, softened
- 3 T. butter, softened
- 1 t. ground cinnamon
- 2 t. salt

Steps:

1. In a glass dish, whisk the heavy whipping cream and vanilla extract for 4 minutes using an electrical beater.
2. In a food blender, whip the coconut oil, cream cheese, and sun butter until combined.
3. Integrate the cocoa powder, ground cinnamon, and butter until the consistency is creamy.
4. Combine the whipped cream into the mixture with a rubber scraper and spoon into a piping bag.
5. Distribute the batter into the silicone mold and top with salt.
6. Freeze overnight or for 6 hours until set and serve.
    Baking Tip:

- If you do not own a piping bag, you can alternatively use a large zip-lock bag. Simply cut the end of one corner of the bottom and you have a do-it-yourself pastry bag!

Cookies & Cream Fat Bomb

This classic recipe will make your mind think you are eating the real deal as they melt in your mouth.

Cooking Time & Total Prep Time: 1-hour 50minutes
Makes: 10 Fat Bombs
Protein: 3 grams
Net Carbs: 0.5 gram
Fat: 8 grams
Sugar: 0 grams
Calories: 93

What you need:

- 2 Scoops cookies and cream protein powder
- One-half a c. coconut oil, melted

- 2 T. cocoa, unsweetened and powder
- One-half c. almond flour
- 2 T. Swerve sweetener, confectioner
- One-eight t. salt
- 2 T. butter, melted

Steps:

1. Set aside silicone cupcake mold.
2. In a saucepan, combine the coconut oil, cookies, and cream protein powder, frequently stirring until thickened.
3. Distribute evenly to the cupcake mold, leaving about a quarter inch at the top of each. Freeze for 30 minutes.
4. Using a hot skillet, empty the almond flour to toast for approximately 3 minutes.
5. Meanwhile, in a glass dish, blend the Swerve, salt, and cocoa powder, whisking to remove all lumpiness.
6. Incorporate the toasted almond flour and melted butter and combine well.

7. Remove the mold and press the crumbly mixture to the tops of the cups.
8. Freeze for one additional hour and serve.

Creamsickle Fat Bomb

Go back to your childhood with this out of the ballpark healthy fat packed treat.

Cooking Time & Total Prep Time: 2 hours 10 minutes
Makes: 10 Fat Bombs
Protein: 1 gram
Net Carbs: 0.7 grams
Fat: 20 grams
Sugar: 0 grams
Calories: 176

What you need:

- 4 oz. heavy cream
- one-half c. coconut oil, melted
- 4 oz. cream cheese
- 1 t. Mio, orange vanilla flavored

- 10 drops Stevia liquid

Steps:

1. Set out a silicone cupcake or candy mold onto the counter.
2. Using a food blender, whip the coconut oil, Mio, heavy cream, Stevia, and cream cheese for 6 minutes until consistency is creamy and smooth.
3. Spoon into the silicone mold and freeze for 2 hours.
4. Serve cold and enjoy!

Iced Coffee Fat Bomb

Perk up your senses and day by having these fat bombs with your morning coffee.

Cooking Time & Total Prep Time: 2 hours 15 minutes
Makes: 15 Fat Bombs
Protein: 1 gram
Net Carbs: 1 gram
Fat: 9 grams
Sugar: 0 grams
Calories: 45

What you need:

- 1 T. instant coffee
- 2 T. Swerve sweetener, confectioner
- 1 T. butter, softened
- 4.5 oz. cream cheese, softened
- 1 T. coconut oil
- 3 t. cocoa, unsweetened and powdered
- 1 T. hot water

Steps:

1. Set ice cube trays or silicone molds onto the counter.
2. Using a food blender, pulse the coffee and Swerve until they are fine powder. Combine the hot water and cream until a paste consistency.
3. Integrate coconut oil, cocoa powder, butter, and cream cheese for approximately 3 minutes.
4. Distribute to the molds or ice cube trays and freeze for 2 hours before serving.
5. Any leftovers can be placed into a freezer safe zip-lock baggie.

Mint Chocolate Chip Fat Bomb

This classic recipe will end up being one of your favorites when you need that quick snack.

Cooking Time & Total Prep Time: 2 hours 10 minutes
Makes: 14 Fat Bombs
Protein: 2 grams
Net Carbs: 1 gram
Fat: 11 grams
Sugar: 0 grams
Calories: 156

What you need:

- 1 t. peppermint extract, sugar-free
- 8 oz. cream cheese
- 1 medium avocado, peeled, pitted and halved
- 2 oz. Swerve sweetener, confectioner
- 1 T. Swerve sweetener, confectioner and separate

- 2 oz. dark chocolate, unsweetened and chopped

Steps:

1. On the counter, place a candy or cupcake mold with 14 cups.
2. Using a food blender, whip the avocado, cream cheese, Swerve, and peppermint extract until combined.
3. Slowly incorporate the dark chocolate into the batter, mixing thoroughly.
4. Transfer the batter to the mold and freeze for 2 hours before serving.
    Variation Tip:

- Alternatively, you can use 1 tablespoon of minced mint in place of the peppermint extract.

Peanut Butter Whip Fat Bomb

When you have the combination of peanut butter and chocolate married together, you simply cannot go wrong.
Cooking Time & Total Prep Time: 1 hour 5 minutes
Makes: 6 Fat Bombs
Protein: 2 grams
Net Carbs: 4 grams
Fat: 26 grams
Sugar: 0 grams
Calories: 259

What you need:

For the fat bombs:

- 12 oz. heavy whipping cream
- 1 t. vanilla extract, sugar-free
- 2 T. peanut butter

For the covering:
- 1 oz. dark chocolate, unsweetened
- 4 oz. heavy whipping cream
- one-half t. Swerve sweetener, confectioner
- 10 drops Stevia liquid
- one-eighth t. vanilla extract, sugar-free

Steps:

1. In a glass dish, whisk the heavy whipping cream and vanilla extract for 4 minutes using an electrical beater.
2. Incorporate the peanut butter and continue to pulse for an additional minute until the consistency is creamy.
3. Spoon the cream mixture into a piping bag and empty into the cupcake mold.
4. Freeze for 2 hours before serving.
5. In a saucepan, boil the 4 ounces of whipping cream and then combine the chocolate. Stir until completely melted together. Remove from heat.
6. Integrate the Swerve, Stevia liquid, and vanilla extract while the mixture is still warm.

7. Cover a flat tray with baking lining and remove the fat bombs from the freezer.
8. Immerse the fat bombs into the cooled covering and move to the prepped tray.
9. Freeze for an additional 60 minutes before serving.

Baking Tip:

- If you do not own a piping bag, you can alternatively use a large zip-lock bag. Simply cut the end of one corner of the bottom and you have a do-it-yourself pastry bag!

Variation Tip:

- If you are dairy intolerant, you may substitute the heavy whipping cream for the same amount of coconut cream, if you desire.

Pumpkin Fat Bomb

Crave to add some fall season into your day? These pumpkin fat bombs are loaded with the healthy fats that you need in your day.
Cooking Time & Total Prep Time: 3 hours 10 minutes
Makes: 6Fat Bombs
Protein: 2 grams
Net Carbs: 4 gram
Fat: 28 grams
Sugar: 1 gram
Calories: 272

What you need:

- 8 oz. cream cheese, softened
- one-half t. pumpkin pie spice
- 4 oz. butter, unsalted and softened
- one-half c. Swerve sweetener, granulated

- 4 oz. pumpkin puree

Steps:

1. Use a silicone cupcake mold or a baking lining covered flat sheet.
2. In a food blender, whip the cream cheese, pumpkin puree, and butter for 2 minutes until a creamy consistency.
3. Incorporate the pumpkin pie spice and Swerve until combined well.
4. If using a mold, distribute the mixture using a piping bag or a regular spoon. Tap the tray lightly on the counter to smooth out the batter.
5. When using the flat sheet, scoop heaping mounds with a cookie scoop.
6. Freeze for 3 hours before serving.
7. Leftovers should be stored in a freezer-safe zip-lock bag or sealed container.

Rocky Road Fat Bomb

You will not be able to tell the difference once you sink your teeth into this classic fat bomb recipe.

Cooking Time & Total Prep Time: 1 hour 40 minutes
Makes: 20 Fat Bombs
Protein: 3 grams
Net Carbs: 2 grams
Fat: 12 grams
Sugar: 1 gram
Calories: 126

What you need:

- 8 oz. cream cheese, softened
- one-half c. almond butter
- 4 oz. dark chocolate chips, unsweetened
- one-third c. Swerve sweetener, granulated

- 2 oz. pecans, raw and chopped
- 1 t. vanilla extract, sugar-free
- 4 oz. butter, unsalted and softened
- one-eight t. salt

Steps:

1. Cover a flat sheet with baking lining or use a non-stick mat.
2. In a food blender, whip the Swerve, cream cheese, and almond butter for approximately one minute.
3. Combine the almond butter, salt, and vanilla extract and pulse for an additional minute.
4. Use a rubber scraper to incorporate the pecans and chocolate chips fully.
5. Refrigerate for approximately 30 minutes. Spoon out 20 individual balls with a cookie scooper and place on the prepped sheet.
6. Freeze for 60 minutes and remove 10 minutes before serving.
7. Any leftovers should be transferred to a freezer bag or a sealed container.

Conclusion

I hope it was fun, informative and provided you with all of the tools you need to add variety to your Keto lifestyle, while giving you more time and money.

www.ingramcontent.com/pod-product-compliance
Lightning Source LLC
Chambersburg PA
CBHW071437070526
44578CB00001B/114